PRAISE FOR
DR. DIAMOND AND BK

"The work described in this book will imprint deeply upon the minds of men for untold generations."

—Alan Shifman Charles, M.D.
Director, Academy of Eastern
Medicine

"Under Dr. Diamond's caring and seemingly tireless direction, Behavioral Kinesiology has taken us farther down the road toward the realization of our highest potential."

—Edgar S. Miller, D.O., F.A.A.O.

"BK is a brilliantly conceived science about the integration of soul, mind, body and environment."

—John Buttrick,
Professor of Music, M.I.T.

"This book represents the efforts of someone who has taken the time to look at man holistically. This is not speculation as far as I am concerned. It is fact, demonstrated in hundreds of scientific laboratories on thousands of subjects."

—Bill Boshears, *Cincinnati Enquirer*

"Dr. John Diamond's valuable contributions in the field of Behavioral Kinesiology offer both professionals and laypersons new, exciting applications in a wide variety of areas related to health restoration and maintainance, as well as preventive medicine."

—Beatric Trum Hunter, author of
The Great Nutrition Robbery

About the Author

Dr. John Diamond graduated cum laude from Sydney University Medical School in 1957, and was awarded the Naughton-Manning Prize for Psychiatry. In Australia, he held many senior clinical and university teaching appointments in clinical psychiatry. After coming to the United States, Dr. Diamond served as an attending psychiatrist at New York's Beth Israel Medical Center and held a professorship of psychiatry at Mount Sinai Medical School, also in New York City. Board certified in psychiatry in both Great Britain and Australia, Dr. Diamond is a member of the Royal Australian and New Zealand College of Psychiatrists and of the Royal College of Psychiatry of Great Britain.

In recent years, Dr. Diamond has expanded his practice to include preventive medicine and currently holds many positions in that field. He is president of the International Academy of Preventive Medicine.

During his twenty-plus years in medicine, Dr. Diamond has lectured to numerous professional organizations, both nationally and internationally. Through the Institute of Behavioral Kinesiology, an organization based in Valley Cottage, New York, Dr. Diamond currently conducts research and teaches the theories and practical applications of BK.

Your Body Doesn't Lie

How to Increase Your Life Energy
Through Behavioral Kinesiology

(original title: BK Behavioral Kinesiology)

John Diamond, M.D.

WARNER BOOKS

A Warner Communications Company

My thanks to
Dr. George Goodheart
for teaching me that
your body doesn't lie.

WARNER BOOKS EDITION

This Warner Books Edition is published by arrangement with Harper & Row, Publishers, Inc.,
10 East 53rd Street,
New York, N.Y. 10022

Book design by Helen Roberts

Warner Books, Inc.,
666 Fifth Avenue,
New York, N.Y. 10103

W A Warner Communications Company

First Warner Books Printing: February, 1980

Reissued: December, 1983

10   9   8   7

Photo Credits

Pages 8, 44, 45, 48, 51, 70, 71, 91, 188: Jim Kalett.

Page 40, T cells, courtesy of Andrejs Liepins, Sloan-Kettering Institute for Cancer Research, New York.

Page 47, top, Cybex Dynamometer, Cybex Division of Lumex, 100 Spence Street, Bayshore, N.Y. 11706.

Page 57, Little girl on beach with outstretched arms, photo by John Pearson, © 1968.

Page 59, Stallion running, from ANIMALS ANIMALS/ © Hope Ryden.

Page 90, Murillo's "The Vision of St. Felix of Cantalicio," Camera Clix.

Page 92, Vincent Van Gogh, "The First Steps." The Metropolitan Museum of Art, Gift of George N. and Helen M. Richard, 1964.

Page 102, Wide palatal arches from *Nutrition and Physical Degeneration* by Weston A. Price, D.D.S., © 1970, courtesy of Price-Pottenger Nutrition Foundation, Inc., P.O. Box 2614, La Mesa, California 92041.

Page 115, Portrait of Juan de Pareja by Diego Rodriguez de Silva y Velázquez. The Metropolitan Museum of Art, Isaac D. Fletcher Fund, Rogers Fund & Bequest of Adelaide Milton de Groot (1876–1967), Bequest of Joseph H. Durkee, by exchange, supplemented by gifts from Friends of the Museum, 1971.

Page 116, Rembrandt's "Head of Christ." The Metropolitan Museum of Art, The Mr. & Mrs. Isaac D. Fletcher Collection, Bequest of Isaac D. Fletcher, 1917.

Page 117, Artist's copy of Velázquez's portrait of Juan de Pareja. Courtesy of The Hispanic Society of America, New York.

Page 118, L.A. Farrah, © Los Angeles Magazine: Cover, April, 1977. Exclusive Licensee: Pro Arts, Inc., Medina, Ohio; Farrah Fawcett Fan Club, Medina, Ohio.

Page 119, Farrah, © 1976 Pro Arts, Inc., Medina, Ohio, USA. All rights reserved.

Page 139, Grant Wood's "American Gothic," courtesy of The Art Institute of Chicago.

Page 152, Toscanini. Reprinted from *This Was Toscanini* by Samuel Antek. Copyright © 1963 by Alice Antek. Photograph copyright © 1963 by Robert Hupka. By permission of Vanguard Press, Inc.

Before You Read
This Book

Perform the following test with a friend or family member serving as subject.

1. Have the subject stand erect, right arm relaxed at his side, left arm held out parallel to the floor with elbow straight as in the picture on the next page.

2. Face the subject and place your left hand on his right shoulder to steady him. Then place your right hand on the subject's extended arm just above the wrist.

3. Tell the subject you are going to try to push his arm down as he resists with all his strength.

4. Now push down on his arm quickly and firmly. The idea is to push just hard enough to test the spring and bounce in the

Fig. 1. Testing the deltoid muscle.

arm, not so hard that the muscle becomes fatigued. It is not a question of who is stronger, but of whether the muscle can lock the shoulder joint against the push.

Was the subject able to resist the pressure? In nearly every case he will be; his arm will remain extended.

Perform the test again as the subject does one of the following things:

- Eats some refined sugar
- Listens to several examples of currently popular music such as the recent hits "Stayin' Alive" by the Bee Gees and Glen Campbell's "Southern Nights."
- Puts a piece of plastic on top of his head (a large Baggie will do nicely)
- Stares at a fluorescent light
- Thinks of an unpleasant situation

The results will be dramatic. In nearly every case the subject will be unable to resist the pressure. His arm will go down easily.

How can this be? Although the tester was pushing with the same amount of pressure as he was before, suddenly the arm has gone weak. It is very much a yes-or-no situation: the arm goes down or it does not.

What has happened? Somehow the refined sugar, or the music, or the other influences have temporarily weakened the arm muscle. The same effect would occur with any other muscle in the body. (We used this particular muscle, the deltoid, because it is convenient to test.) Thus it is apparent that, under the test conditions, something has gone wrong with the energy supply throughout the body. What has gone wrong and what we can learn from this is the subject of this book.

Contents

Acknowledgments

I wish to thank all my teachers, contemporary and ancient, in preventive medicine, psychiatry, the humanities, and Applied Kinesiology. And, of course, to my greatest teachers—my students and patients—a warm thank you. I also wish to salute my fellow members of the International Academy of Preventive Medicine.

For her cheerful and unselfish help in so many ways, I wish to express my gratitude to Victoria Galban. Joe Gould deserves a special thanks for his persevering desire to perfect many of the illustrations in this book. Thanks also to Jim Kalett for his excellent photographs on BK testing, to Virginia Rohan for her helpful assistance, and to my Alexander teacher, Christina Wilton, for her inspiration and patient teaching.

13

For all her kind advice during the writing of this book, I wish to thank my editor, Jeanne Flagg. And for his enthusiasm and confidence, thanks to Irv Levey, Director, Barnes & Noble Books.

For her dedication to my work and to this book, my deepest gratitude to my wife, Betty, without whom this book could never have been written. She deserves more thanks than I can possibly express.

John Diamond, M.D.
July 1978

Foreword

Dr. John Diamond has revolutionized preventive medicine. His holistic approach to the individual is so thorough that no stimulus, no influence passes without examination. When I was President of the International Academy of Preventive Medicine, I saw the variety and depth of the applications of Behavioral Kinesiology. A philosophy as well as an integrated science, BK spans all the healing arts and has been incorporated into such diverse areas as psychosomatic medicine, allergy, acupuncture, psychiatry, sports training, nutrition, dentistry, osteopathy, and so on.

BK has profoundly changed my personal life. It has also made gratifying changes in my profession, which is dentistry. No one needs to be reminded of the feelings of apprehension and even of fear that accompany a visit to a dental office. The dentist is concerned not only about the discomfort of his patients but also about his own performance—doing a complex job in a small working space. These stresses take their toll. Dentists have one of the highest divorce and suicide rates in the professions.

But these last few years have been very different for me. Dr. Diamond has shown those of us in the healing arts how to "center" our energies and those of our patients. He has taken the distress out of stress for doctor, staff, and patients. Ever since I incorporated his techniques into my practice, treatment has progressed smoothly, without fear and anxiety. And the reward for me is more energy, less stress, and, best of all, a new sense of well-being.

BK has also revolutionized many psychiatric practices and even psychiatric hospitals. Dr. David Hawkins, Medical Director of the North Nassau Mental Health Center and President of the American Academy of Orthomolecular Psychiatry, has said that by employing the principles of BK he has been able to transform entire psychiatric wards. Dr. Alan Shifman Charles, Director of the Academy of Eastern Medicine, sees BK as the "first pure method of understanding and discovering disease on a multi-centric level," replacing the need for sensitive and expensive equipment. And Dr. Edgar Miller, a prominent osteopath of Concord, Massachusetts, considers Dr. Diamond's work to be "a rich source of new ideas which not only in-form but curiously fashion themselves into a powerful teaching tool for the healing arts." BK, he says, "has given me a much broader understanding of the countless forces that act to disturb the harmony that is essential to health and has shown me how to assess their effects. Under Dr. Diamond's caring and seemingly tireless direction, BK has taken us farther down the road toward the realization of our highest potential."

The applications of BK are not limited to the healing professions. Many musicians, for example, have discovered startling benefits. One eminent Professor of Music, John Buttrick of M.I.T., has written that BK principles "allow a new mastery over physical resources, performance stress, and artistic medium." Those who exercise or participate in sports events find many beneficial applications, too. Jeff Wilcox of the Sports Training Institute of New York City, enthusiastically recommends BK as part of a total body fitness program, and we've just scratched the surface of the sports applications.

For a curator at the Metropolitan Museum of Art, BK has opened up numerous new perspectives in the whole field of art— painting, sculpture, and architecture. She says, "Insights I have obtained into art appreciation and understanding of the artistic creative impulse and of aesthetic criticism have been of inestimable value."

One of the many important applications of BK to our daily life is in the field of nutrition. Many prominent nutritionists see it as

an invaluable tool in assessing the effects of
various foods. Beatrice Trum Hunter, author
of *The Great Nutrition Robbery*, has written
that "John Diamond's valuable contributions
in the field of Behavioral Kinesiology offer
both professionals and laypersons new, exciting applications in a wide variety of areas related to health restoration and maintenance,
as well as preventive medicine." Another
well-known nutritionist, Dr. Hans Kugler,
author of *Your First 100 Years of Health*,
speaks highly of Dr. Diamond's seminars
across the country, "Dr. Diamond," he says,
"gets enthusiastically involved to a degree
that is only possible for someone who knows
that what he is talking about is something
truly new and exciting."

I have mentioned here just a few of the
applications of BK. Dr. Diamond's breadth of
scope and compelling desire to help his fellow man have enabled him to give us powerful new insights into ourselves and others.
His brilliantly conceived new science will
change your life as it has changed mine. His
work on the thymus gland alone is a valuable
contribution which will be remembered for
generations.

BK is the first line of prevention. You examine your body at an energy level, long before physical problems develop. You look at
your life-style, at the influences in your surroundings, at your attitudes in a new light,
and with a deeper respect. You find yourself
doing things not to prevent disease but to increase your level of health. As Dr. Diamond

says, the ultimate goal of BK is the achievement of Positive Health—the raising of energy, the excitement and the power that come with true wellness. In this regard BK is the promise of the future.

—Jerome Mittelman, D.D.S.
Past President, International
Academy of Preventive Medicine

"Do not inflate plain things into marvels, but reduce marvels to plain things."

—Bacon

"These assertions I make deliberately, after careful weighing and consideration, in no spirit of dispute or momentary zeal; but from strong and convinced feeling, and with a consciousness of being able to prove them."

—John Ruskin

Your Body Doesn't Lie

(1)

Introduction

"Every man, woman and child holds the possibility of physical perfection: it rests with each of us to attain it by personal understanding and effort."

—*F. M. Alexander*

Stand at a busy intersection and look at the people passing by. Are they walking upright and proud with a spring in their steps, alertness in their faces, and rhythm in their movements? Or are they plodding along with head bowed, shoulders rounded, and chest collapsed? I think you will find that most of these people seem like prisoners on the earth, overwhelmed by gravity, rather than buoyant creatures, full of the joy of existence.

When we see an animal that does not walk proud and erect and full of life, we immediately think that there is something wrong with it. Yet we do not feel any concern for the weary and dejected people we see on Main Street. What we would consider an unhealthy condition in animals we call normal in human beings. It is not normal, it is *average*. When someone full of energy and life walks down the street, we turn and stare as if this were a rarity. It is the *normal* condition.

Just as it is not normal for us to walk slumped and joyless, it is not normal for us to get sick or die from chronic degenerative diseases. Most males in our society expect that sooner or later they will have a heart attack. Most of us fear that we will get cancer or, if we manage to escape that dread disease, that we will fall victim in old age to arthritis, diabetes, blindness, or severe mental impairment. This need not be. The long-lived people of the highlands of southern Ecuador rarely develop these diseases. Nor do they lose their eyesight or become arthritic in old age. David Davies, who spent some time with these remarkable people, observed that they were slim, lucid, and agile, and had great passion for life. "If you were walking behind a man," he observed, "until you caught up with him you would not know if he was 40 or 120, such was the nature of their walk. . . . There was something dynamic—even tigerlike—about their movements. . . ."*

*David Davies, *The Centenarians of the Andes* (New York: Anchor Press/Doubleday; London: Barrie & Jenkins, Ltd., 1975), p. 51

We may not be able to adopt the simple diet, the high level of activity, and the simple way of life of these people of the Andes, but we can do much to prevent chronic diseases from developing. I have come to believe that all illness starts as a problem on the *energy level*, a problem that may exist for many years before it manifests itself in physical disease. It appears that a generalized reduction of body energy leads to energy imbalances in particular parts of the body. If we become aware of these energy imbalances when they first occur, we have a long grace period in which to correct them. We will then be practicing primary prevention.

Most prevention practiced nowadays is secondary prevention. "I've had a heart attack—prevent me from having another." "I've got an ulcer—keep it from getting worse." With primary prevention the problems are still at an energy level; there is no gross pathological change. Therefore we can expect a return to normal when the energy imbalance is corrected. If we practice primary prevention, we will live as we are supposed to live, and grow old as we are supposed to grow old, and die as we are supposed to die, not go through life from one illness to another, losing vitality and the will to live, and then dying the ignoble sort of death we now die in cold hospitals. Like the centenarians of the Andes and the Caucasus, we will work hard and find simple pleasures, free of illness, all the days of our lives, gradu-

ally getting older and slower until one day
we just pass on.

> He bade, his hundred and first year at end,
> Diggers and carpenters make grave
>   and coffin;
> Saw that the grave was deep,
>   the coffin sound,
> Summoned the generations of his house,
> Lay in the coffin, stopped his breath
>   and died.*

I have always thought of psychiatry as a
form of preventive medicine. If mental stress
is relieved, physical illness has much less
chance of developing. However, I practiced
psychiatry for a number of years before I
found a really effective means of using primary prevention in helping my patients.
Early in my internship I realized that most of
my patients wanted only to be relieved of
any symptoms that were causing them difficulty—pain, limping, and so forth—so that
they could go back to the poor health habits
they had before. So few seemed to want to
change, to be really well. This was the bitter
disappointment I faced day after day.

I remember the sad case of a very attrac-
tive woman of about forty, a former flight at-
tendant, who married a thrice-divorced big-
business executive who treated her like an
ornament. Her role was to be pretty and po-

*From Yeats's "In Tara's Halls." Reprinted with permis-
sion of Macmillan Publishing Co., Inc., from *Collected Poems*
by William Butler Yeats. Copyright 1940 by Georgie Yeats, re-
newed 1968 by Bertha Georgie Yeats, Michael Butler Yeats
and Anne Yeats.

lite. and a perfect hostess. She wasn't to express herself, to be a person in her own right. During the course of her marriage she developed one psychosomatic illness after another. By the time I saw her, she had been to numerous psychiatrists. Whenever I tried to discuss with her her degrading role, her self-debasement, she would cut off the conversation. She would never face it. Eventually she told her husband of my feelings about this, and then, of course, he removed her from therapy. When I heard of her next, she was receiving electroshock therapy for depression and was spending months at a time in a hospital.

In spite of such discouraging cases, in all my years of practice only one of my patients—and I had thousands—committed suicide. It was not my psychiatric ability, I knew, that was keeping these patients alive. It was something else. I was not achieving more "cures" than other psychiatrists. What I was doing was investing great amounts of myself in each patient. These people were improving and staying well because of me, because of my energy, because of what I was doing, not because of changes taking place within *them*. In essence, they hadn't changed, they were just being buttressed up by me.

With my psychosomatic patients my role was clearly that of mother hen. By taking these patients under my wing, I could help prevent the destructive or, at best, ultimately inconsequential treatments that they were undergoing. For example, once the gynecologist knew that I, the psychiatrist, had the patient, he was less likely to do a hysterectomy. Once the allergist knew that I was seeing his patient, he felt he could reduce the amount of asthma medication. What I was doing was literally buying time for the patient—time in which he could sort out things for himself.

But how was I to give back to my patients the responsibility for being well? I could talk to them and demonstrate and help them evaluate the extent to which their relationships with others were affecting them. But I could never get it through to them that their well-being was really their responsibility.

Although they were dependent on me, some of my patients did seem to gain a better understanding of their problems. However, I soon noticed a strange thing: the longer they remained in therapy, the more depressed and devitalized they became. Even I was becoming depressed and tired. I remember well how I used to slump in my chair, sinking lower and lower as the day went on; how I was drinking more and more coffee and eating more and more sugar in a vain attempt to raise my energy. The truth was unescapable: I was giving my patients more understanding and knowledge, but somehow lowering their energy and mine in the process. I knew I could no longer go on doing what I was doing, but I didn't know where to go or what to do.

After months of deliberation, I decided to try a new approach. From now on I would not treat psychiatric problems as such, but would deal with them in relation to physical conditions. I would practice preventive medicine, which meant raising the patient's energy to overcome the earliest manifestations of disease or, better yet, to prevent disease from occurring in the first place. A whole new area of treatment opened up. I became interested in nutrition and natural supplements, and made a new appraisal of routine medical and psychiatric medications in relation to body energy. I also investigated various types of physical and postural therapies. Now, I thought, I would be able to treat my patients much more completely than ever before. I was out of the more narrow psychiatric framework and into what we may call a general preventive, energy-raising type of practice.

However, I soon realized the limitations of what I was doing. I was dealing in generalities. I had to get down to *this* body. I had to find out what *this* body needed done.

The answer came unexpectedly. I happened to meet a friend who told me of an interesting lecture he had attended, in which muscle-testing was used. Although I had never heard of this work before, I had a strong feeling that this was what I was looking for. The lecturer was Dr. George Goodheart, the originator of a specialty called Applied Kinesiology. I lost no time in making contact with him. This was the be-

ginning of a firm friendship and a close working relationship. Dr. Goodheart had been
working with Applied Kinesiology for fifteen
or so years. What he had discovered was that
each large muscle relates to a body organ. A
weakness in a muscle usually means that
there is a problem at the energy level in the
associated organ. Indeed, by treating the
muscle in a variety of ways and making it
strong again, he was able to improve the
functioning of the organ as well.

Over the years, Dr. Goodheart had
achieved many amazing results—results that
had far-reaching implications. For the first
time, nutrition made sense. If a particular
nutritional supplement was given to a patient and the muscle tested strong, it was the
right supplement for that patient; if the muscle remained weak, it was not. Other meth-
ods of treatment could be similarly evalu-
ated. With Applied Kinesiology, doctors had
a really useful therapeutic tool, a system of
feedback from the body itself. If they gave a
patient the proper treatment, the body
would respond immediately as if to say, "Yes,
that is what was needed."

This was Dr. Goodheart's great advance.
I became very excited about this and studied
his work carefully. Then I began to adapt it
to my own practice. Goodheart's techniques
involved a great deal of physical manipula-
tion and were better suited for patients with
specific physical problems than for those
who needed treatment of a more holistic nature. My patients fell in the latter category.

Now I was truly practicing democratic medicine. No longer was it what I in my "great and exalted" position as doctor or what the even more exalted textbook said should be done. It was what the body said I should do. And when I did things right, the body told me so. The patient's response determined the treatment.

Best of all, I was now in a position to give back to my patients the responsibility for being well. Instead of submitting humbly to my treatment, they were sharing fully in it. Moreover, they were seeing themselves in a new light. It is an emotional experience to gain insight. And kinesiological testing is an emotional experience. It is an "ah-ha" experience, and it is only through this kind of experience that we arrive at sudden truths.

My own research and practice led in time to the separate but related discipline of Behavioral Kinesiology (BK), an integration of psychiatry, psychosomatic medicine, Kinesiology, preventive medicine, and the humanities. Its culmination is the present book, which, with a few exceptions, consists of my original research findings.

Behavioral Kinesiology uses the basic testing techniques of Applied Kinesiology, but focuses on the factors in the patient's surroundings and life-style that are raising and lowering body energy. Many of the factors that lower energy are products of the technological revolution: the poisons and noises in our environment, the overrefined and unnatural foods we find on the supermarket shelves, the synthetic fabrics from which so many of our clothes are made. Other factors are individual habits or tendencies, such as posture, ability to handle stress, and human relationships.

In the following pages I will show you how to determine the extent to which various factors in your environment and in your life-style are affecting your body energy. I will suggest many energy-enriching activities you can substitute for energy-depleting ones. And I will show you how to modify or counteract the effect of those debilitating factors that cannot be entirely eliminated. But first you must know something about the role of the thymus gland in kinesiological testing and its relation to body energy—indeed, to our Life Energy.

(2)

The Mysterious Thymus Gland

"Has it yet fallen to the lot of any writer upon the thymus to write the truth and be believed?"

—*Beard, 1902*

The thymus gland lies just beneath the upper part of the breastbone in the middle of the chest. It is present in all mammals, and is called the sweetbread in calves. Until the 1950s little was understood about the thymus, although there had been clues to its function for many years. As far back as 1902, Foulerton, a London physician, was using thymus extract in the treatment of cancer. However, the standard teaching was that the thymus gland had no function at all in the adult, a delusion fostered by the fact that during autopsy the thymus was usually found to be quite small and atrophied. This is because the thymus gland, in response to acute stress such as an infection, can shrivel to half its size in twenty-four hours. No wonder it was in a state of atrophy when examined post-mortem!

The fact that the size of the thymus was generalized from autopsy observations led to a tragic misdiagnosis of illness in children in the 1920s to the 1940s. It was known from routine autopsies that children have larger thymuses than adults. However, when children who died suddenly, as in "crib death," were found at post-mortem examination to have particularly large thymus glands, they were thought to have died from a thymus-related disease, a disease given the name "status thymicolymphaticus."

Research on the thymus gland in the 1950s, along with further evidence from post-mortem examination, brought this disease into question. Pathologists took note of the fact that battlefield autopsies during the Korean War revealed that soldiers who died in battle had larger thymus glands than men of the same age who died from chronic illness in a hospital. Eventually it was realized that the thymus shrinks rapidly during serious illness or great physical stress. The children who had died from "status thymicolymphaticus" had died before the gland had had time to shrink; their large thymuses were actually the normal size. A whole disease had been constructed on the erroneous idea that the thymus gland had swollen and caused death. To think that children's thymus glands had frequently been irradiated to make them smaller on the assumption that this would reduce the chance of illness! What it did was destroy a vital part of their immune system and make them susceptible to infections, cancer, and chronic diseases!

In spite of modern research findings, the myth of the shriveling useless thymus dies hard. Whenever I lecture on the thymus gland to medical audiences, I am reminded that "everyone knows that the thymus gland has no function in adult life." But the evidence accumulated over the last twenty years on the thymus gland's role in immunology is so overwhelming that it is hard for me to believe that there is not some unconscious factor working to deny it the recognition due to it.

In a human being or an animal in which the thymus gland has been removed or destroyed, there is a loss in effectiveness of the immune mechanisms of the body that guard against infection and cancerous growth. For example, if a young rat that has had its thymus removed is injected with cancer cells, the cancer will take over and the rat will die. However, if the thymus gland is intact, the tumor will be recognized as a hostile invader and will be rejected. There is now considerable evidence that enhancement of the immune response by administering thymus extract can overcome some forms of clinical cancer. A search of the literature shows, as I stated above, that thymus extract was used clinically for the treatment of cancer as long ago as 1902.

In embryonic and early life the thymus gland is vitally concerned with growth, as has been demonstrated by the fact that administration of thymus extract dramatically increases growth rate in laboratory animals. More importantly, it is the "school and factory"* for lymphocytes—the white blood cells responsible for the immunological reactions in the body. Lymphocytes, in an immature state, come to the thymus from the bone marrow. Under the influence of thymus hormones, these cells mature, then leave the thymus and settle in the lymph nodes and the spleen, where they give rise to other generations of lymphocytes called T cells (T for thymus-derived). Thymus hormones travel through the bloodstream and continue to exert their influence over the departed T cells. Thus, the thymus can be considered to be a true endocrine gland—that is, an organ that secretes a hormone into the bloodstream to be carried to another part of the body where it will have its effect.

We know that the thymus continues to secrete hormones and to "train" and export T cells until late in life. After puberty it diminishes in size because it is no longer concerned with growth. Any further shrinkage is due to stress and other factors to be discussed in this book.

The thymus gland, then, prepares the T

*G. J. V. Nossal, *Antibodies and Immunity*, 2nd ed. (New York: Basic Books, 1978), p. 97.

cell to do its work—to distinguish self from not self, friend from foe, and to destroy foreign cells. This role, called immunological surveillance, is directly concerned with resistance to infections and cancer.

A recent case described in a medical journal is that of a young boy who was admitted to the hospital in coma from a severe viral pneumonia. He was unconscious, with a high temperature, and was on forced respiration, being unable to breathe unassisted. Everything was done to resuscitate him, but it was quite obvious that he was going to die. The equivalent of a T-cell count was performed; approximately one fifth the normal level was found. He was then given an injection of thymus extract, and within twenty-four hours the entire process had reversed itself. His temperature was down, he was breathing unassisted, and he was conscious. This is the kind of dramatic recovery we are going to see more and more as accurate testing of thymus function and administration of thymus extract, when indicated, becomes routine in medical practice, as I am sure it will in the next five or ten years. As one of the most eminent workers in the field has said, "The second golden age of 'thymology' is just beginning."*

Probably the most acceptable theory of cancer is that formulated by Sir MacFarlane Burnet,† the Australian Nobel Prize winner. Of the billions of new cells produced in the

*J. F. A. P. Miller, *Lancet*, December 16, 1967, p. 1302.

†F. M. Burnet, *Immunology, Aging, and Cancer* (San Francisco: W. H. Freeman and Company, 1976).

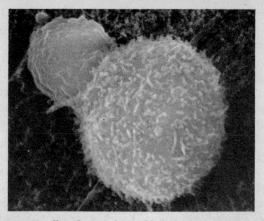

Above, a T cell, a thymus-derived lymphocyte, attacks a cancer cell (large sphere), which it identifies by the antigen molecules protruding from its surface. Below, the cancer cell is dying indicated by the deep folds in its surface membrane. These micrographs were made by Andrejs Liepins of the Sloan-Kettering Institute for Cancer Research.

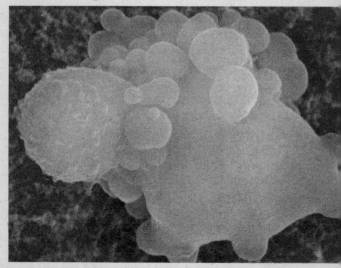

Fig. 2.

body each day, some will be abnormal. One of the functions of the T cells is to recognize these abnormal cells and destroy them. However, if the T cells are not activated by the thymus hormone, the abnormal cells may "take" and develop into clinical cancer. Hence the critical role of the thymus gland throughout adult life in the prevention of cancer.

Now we begin to understand why cancer increases with age. It has been shown that the antibody response of old mice is only about 5 percent that of young mice. Old mice cannot reject cancer cells injected into them. However, if old mice are given thymus hormone at the same time, cancer does not develop. In all mammalian species there is a falling off in thymus activity with advancing years, and a corresponding increase in the rate of cancer. The more we can stimulate thymus activity throughout life, the greater will be our ability to ward off cancer.

The dramatic atrophy of the thymus gland in a person undergoing stress is not fully understood. Within a day of severe injury or sudden illness, millions of lymphocytes are destroyed and the thymus shrinks to half its size. This is part of the general reaction to stress described by Hans Selye.*

We will be considering various types of stress throughout this book. Our concern now is the role of the thymus gland in BK testing.

---

*Hans Selye, *Stress Without Distress* (New York: J. B. Lippincott Company, 1974).

(3)

BK Testing

"A wise man ought to realize that health is his most valuable possession and learn how to treat his illnesses by his own judgment."

—*Hippocrates*

Let's review the testing technique described at the beginning of this book.*

As you will recall, it takes two people to perform a kinesiological test. Choose a friend or a family member for testing. We'll call him or her your subject.

1. Have the subject stand erect, right

*The muscle testing outlined in this chapter is a modified version of that described in the classic work *Muscles: Testing and Function* by Henry O. Kendall et al. (Baltimore: Williams & Wilkins, 2nd ed., 1971).

arm relaxed at his side, left arm held out parallel to the floor, elbow straight.*

2. Face the subject and place your left hand on his right shoulder to steady him. Then place your right hand on the subject's extended left arm just above the wrist. (See Figures 3 and 4.)

3. Tell the subject you are going to try to push his arm down as he resists with all his strength.

4. Now push down on his arm fairly quickly, firmly, and evenly. The idea is to push just hard enough to test the spring and bounce in the arm, not so hard that the muscle becomes fatigued. It is not a question of who is stronger, but of whether the muscle can "lock" the shoulder joint against the push.

NOTE: *Do not smile* when you are conducting a BK test or are being tested yourself. (See Chapter 6.)

Unless there is some physical problem with the muscle, it will test strong. Assuming it does, give your subject a little refined sugar to eat and test again. In nearly every case his muscle will test weak; although you are pushing down no harder than before, the muscle will not be able to resist the pressure and the subject's arm will fall to his side.

What has happened? Somehow the refined sugar has reduced the energy supply in the subject's body, as reflected by the fact

---

*You may use the other arm if you wish.

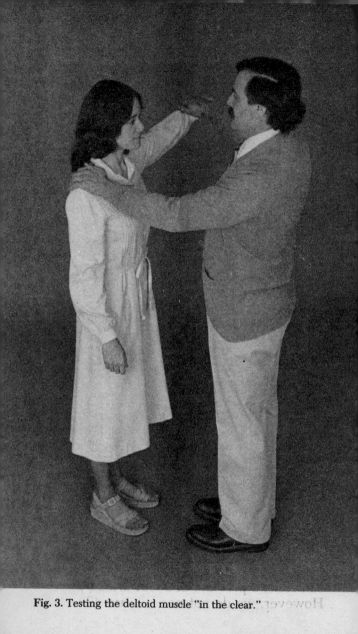

Fig. 3. Testing the deltoid muscle "in the clear."

Fig 4. Closeup of BK muscle testing "in the clear."

that the muscle has lost strength. The same
effect would occur with any other muscle in
the body. We are testing this particular muscle, the middle part of the deltoid, because it
is the easiest muscle to test. This muscle, as
any other muscle, is an indicator of the
body's energy supply. Hence, a single muscle
used for BK testing is called an *indicator
muscle*.

A device that measures muscle strength,
called a kinesiometer (Figure 5), shows that a
strong muscle can withstand up to 40 pounds
of pressure, whereas a muscle that is weak
can resist a pressure of about fifteen pounds.
However, we do not need to use 40 pounds

of pressure each time we test muscle strength, because we develop a feel for whether the muscle is strong enough to "lock" the joint or not. We are looking for the spring in the muscle. And when it is not there, when the muscle is weak, the difference is obvious both to the tester and to the person being tested.

Let's go back to your subject. Test his indicator muscle just as you did before. It should be strong. Now have your subject place the fingertips of his free hand on the skin over the point where the second rib joins the breastbone (the sternomanubrial joint). This point, shown in Figure 7, is directly over the thymus gland. Now, with your subject touching the thymus point, test the indicator muscle again (Figure 8). Is it still strong, or has it gone weak? Suppose it

Fig 5. The Bio-My kinesiometer, used in muscle testing.

The Cybex Dynamometer, another device used in muscle test-ing. Even the quadriceps, perhaps the strongest muscle in the body, shows a reduction to about half strength when a weak-ening stimulus is introduced. The tracing in the graph below shows the results of testing the quadriceps and hamstring muscles with and without stimulus. The first two peaks (left, quadriceps, right, hamstring) represent the strength of these muscles when tested "in the clear." Maximum strength is 66 foot-pounds of pressure. The second set of peaks represent the strength of the same two muscles when the body energy sup-ply is decreased by a negative stimulus. Maximum strength is now only 36 foot-pounds of pressure. The third set of peaks, obtained when the two muscles are tested again with the stimulus removed, shows that strength has returned.

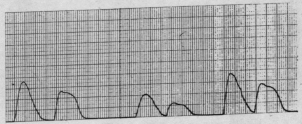

Fig 6.

Fig 7. The thymus test-touch point. The fingers must be touching the skin.

has gone weak. What has happened is this: You have found a muscle, called an indicator muscle, to be strong "in the clear"—that is, without the subject's touching any part of his body with his free hand. But when you had the subject put his hand on the point in question, the indicator muscle tested weak. In BK, this means either that the energy supply to the subject's thymus gland is insufficient or that his thymus gland is underactive at the moment. If his indicator muscle remained strong on touching the thymus point, there was no kinesiological evidence of an energy imbalance involving his thymus gland at that time.

Three results are possible:

1. You are not affected by the stimulus.
2. The stimulus weakens the thymus gland.
3. The stimulus is so detrimental that the muscle tests weak without test-touching the thymus.

I therefore recommend that when testing for all the factors mentioned in this book, you test both in the clear and by test-touching the thymus.

If a test involving the thymus test point calls for a strong thymus at the start and your subject's thymus tests weak, you can temporarily activate it by tapping it lightly two or three times. Don't tap it too vigorously, however; if you do, his thymus may be strengthened, although temporarily, to such a degree that you can't demonstrate the test involved.

You are well on the path to positive health when your thymus, without special activation, tests strong even when confronted by the noxious influences presented in this book. In my practice, at the end of each session or interview, I always test my patients and students with some negative factor such as the rock beat. If they test weak, I know that further strengthening of the thymus is needed.

How do we know it is the thymus gland that we are testing? All we need to do is to have the subject chew one tablet of thymus extract. Instantly the indicator muscle will become strong. Other extracts will not have this effect.

This test-touch process—touching with one hand while an indicator muscle is being tested—is called by kinesiologists "therapy localization." How it works is not well understood. Perhaps some energy circuit is completed to the point in the body that was low in energy. We do not know.*

Try this test: Instead of having your subject test-touch the thymus point, have him test-touch other places on the body at random. In other words, test the indicator muscle each time your subject touches a different point. Chances are that touching these other points will not cause the indicator mus-

*It's tempting to offer explanations for the phenomena described in this book. However, I have kept them to a minimum. This work is new, and to formulate theories at this stage would be premature and limiting.

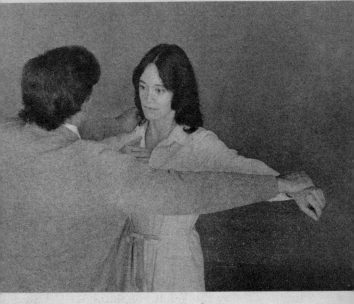

Fig. 8. Test-touching the thymus gland

cle to go weak. It is where the fingertips are placed—the exact test-touch position—that is critical. A weak muscle reaction to test-touching shows that this specific point on your subject's body is functioning under the stress of an energy imbalance.

Now, if your subject's thymus gland point tested weak, merely thump this area ten or twelve times and have your subject test-touch that point again. After thumping, the indicator muscle will usually test strong. The thymus gland has been activated, albeit only temporarily. Your subject's body is now saying that that point is okay, that it is now

testing clear, free of energy disturbances.
You have asked your subject's body the question, "Is something wrong with that point?"
and the body has said, "Yes, there is." You
have then done the appropriate thing to correct the energy flow at that point, for your
subject's body has said, "Thank you. It is
fixed." It is not a question of any "expert"
saying that *this* is what is wrong or that *that*
is what is wrong. The body's response to the
test-touching procedure gives you the answer. The body knows! We have only to
know how to ask.

Suppose your subject's thymus gland
point tested strong on the test-touching you
performed initially. Test again to confirm
this result. Now have him think of some catastrophe, such as being in an automobile accident. Test again. What has happened? Usually, if not invariably, the thymus gland will
test weak. Next, ask your subject to think of
someone he hates. The thymus gland will
probably continue to test weak. But now ask
him to think of someone he loves. Instantly
the gland will test strong! You can see how
quickly we can learn significant things about
the mind and the body by BK testing.

For full kinesiological testing, we test
most of the muscles in the body. However, in
this introductory book we will use only one
indicator muscle, the middle deltoid. Also,
well over 100 points on the body are used in
test-touching (therapy localization) for full diagnosis and treatment. Here we will restrict
ourselves almost entirely to the thymus

gland test point. From that one test point a great deal can be discovered that can be of enormous benefit to you in your daily life. The thymus gland is the first organ to be affected by stress, as you have learned. It is also the seat of our Life Energy, which is the subject of the next chapter.

(4)

Your Life Energy

" . . . the pleasure afforded by every organic form
is in proportion to its appearance of healthy vital
energy."

—*John Ruskin*

Our Life Energy is the source of our physical
and mental well-being, of glowing health, of
the joy of living. Throughout recorded history it has had many names. Hippocrates
called it the Vis Medicatrix Naturae, the
healing power of nature. Paracelsus called it
the Archaeus; the Chinese, Ch'i; the Egyptians, Ka; the Hindus, Prana; the Hawaiians,
Mana. It is all the same thing.

Several years ago I was delighted to
come across a discussion of the "symptoms"
of health in a book published in 1853. "Our
medical books," wrote Dr. Nichols, "are

filled with descriptions, symptoms, and causes of disease. I wish, if possible, to give a clear description, enumerate the symptoms, and guide my reader to a knowledge of the conditions of Health." Here are his "symptoms":

HEALTH, in a human being, is the perfection of bodily organization, intellectual energy, and moral power.

HEALTH is the fullest expression of all the faculties and passions of man, acting together in perfect harmony.

HEALTH is entire freedom from pain of body and discordance of mind.

HEALTH is beauty, energy, purity, holiness, happiness.

HEALTH is that condition in which man is the highest known expression of the power and goodness of his Maker.

When a man is perfect in his own nature, body, and soul, perfect in their harmonious adaptations and action, and living in perfect harmony with nature, with his fellow man, and with God, he may be said to be in a state of HEALTH.*

There has never been a more magnificent description of health than Walt Whitman's, which he called "Health (Old Style)."

In that condition the whole body is elevated to a state by others unknown—inwardly and outwardly illuminated, purified, made solid, strong, yet buoyant. A singular charm, more than beauty, flickers out of, and over, the face—a curious transparency beams in the eyes, both in the iris

---

*T. L. Nichols, *Esoteric Anthropology* (New York: Stringer & Townsend, 1853), p. 227.

and the white—the temper partakes also. . . . The play of the body in motion takes a previously unknown grace. Merely *to move* is then a happiness, a pleasure—to breathe, to see, is also. All the beforehand gratifications, drink, spirits, coffee, grease, stimulants, mixtures, late hours, luxuries, deeds of the night, seem as vexatious dreams, and now the awakening;—many fall into their natural places, wholesome, conveying diviner joys.*

Such a glorious state of health as Whitman describes springs from an abundant Life Energy. It is rare indeed. But do not be discouraged. Even if you have been ill and fatigued, you can do much to increase your Life Energy. Increasing your Life Energy, however, does not mean giving yourself a temporary "lift" such as you would experience from eating sugar, nor does it mean working up to a state of "nervous" energy. Rather, it means increasing the life force within you—your vitality. Vitality is not necessarily activity. Just look at a healthy animal at rest and you will know that that animal has a high degree of Life Energy.

By testing the thymus gland point as outlined in the preceding chapter, you can determine whether your Life Energy is high or low. Unfortunately, about 95 percent of the general population tests low on the Life Energy scale. There are many reasons for this, as the following chapters will reveal. The point I want to make here is this: I have

*Walt Whitman, *The Complete Poetry and Prose of Walt Whitman*, as prepared by him for the Deathbed Edition, Vol. II (Garden City, N.Y.: Garden City Books, 1954), p. 513.

Fig. 9. The Vital Life Energy of a Child.

never seen a patient with a chronic degenerative illness who did not have an underactive thymus gland. Now, certainly the fear and discouragement engendered by the illness can account for the thymus's testing weak. However, I believe that it is the thymus weakness, or underactivity, that is the original cause of the illness. *All illnesses start with a diminution of the Life Energy.* Should this decrease continue, some organ of the body will be the target for the illness.

Thus, if we can achieve optimum thymus gland functioning and maintain it (assuming we don't already have too many fixed pathological conditions), we should have before us a much healthier, happier, and longer life than would otherwise be the case.

The ancient Chinese envisioned the Life Energy, which they call Ch'i, as flowing through the body in a system of pathways. Twelve main pathways, or meridians, were recognized, each related to a specific body organ for which it was named. These meridians, which are paired, are Bladder, Circulation-Sex, Gall Bladder, Heart, Kidney, Large Intestine, Liver, Lung, Small Intestine, Spleen, Stomach, and Triple Heater (Thyroid). Ch'i enters the body with the air that is breathed and the food and water that are swallowed. The flow is continuous, from one meridian to another in a certain sequence. In the practice of acupuncture, an energy imbalance in a particular meridian can be determined and then corrected by the insertion of needles at specific points along the meridians. The needling of these points balances the energy flow in that meridian and has a therapeutic effect on the associated organ.

Although the Chinese acupuncture system of treatment has worked to great benefit for centuries, attempts to fit it into Western medicine have not been satisfactory. The problem is that the acupuncture system does not seem to follow known anatomical pathways. Dr. Felix Mann, one of the great West-

Fig.10. You can see that this mustang is full of energy. His motion is fluid and free, his posture excellent. Test the effect of this photograph. You will find it energy-enhancing.

Fig. 11. The vitality of this animal is apparent even at rest. He is ready for action if required. This photograph, too, is strengthening.

ern practitioners of the ancient Chinese art, feels that the flow of Ch'i along the meridians may be a wave of electrical depolarization traveling along fibers of the autonomic nervous system.* Despite the claims of a North Korean doctor in the 1960s, no special system of ducts has been identified.

Because there are no known structures that serve as acupuncture pathways, Western physicians are not inclined to regard the body as a source and conductor of electromagnetic energy. And it is at this level that the acupuncture system is to be conceptualized. The meridians are the major channels that conduct electromagnetic energy throughout the body. Whenever there is an energy imbalance in a particular meridian system, the organs associated with that system will not function properly.

Now, it was Dr. George Goodheart's brilliant discovery that there is a direct relationship between muscles and meridians. A weak muscle indicates an energy imbalance—a Ch'i imbalance—in the organ related to that muscle via the appropriate acupuncture meridian. Muscles, then, can be thought of as energy pumps that increase the flow of energy through specific meridians when the thymus gland is functioning correctly. When the thymus is not, the energy flow will be decreased. This explains why, when we do BK muscle-testing, we're not testing the mechanical strength of the muscle as is done,

*Felix Mann, *The Meridians of Acupuncture* (London: William Heinemann Medical Books, 1964), p. 13.

say, by a physical therapist. Rather, what we are testing is the energy in the meridian associated with that muscle, and the ability of the body to replenish the energy. So, when we test a specific muscle, we are putting stress on the related meridian. If the flow of energy to that meridian has already been disrupted, then the energy level within the meridian will fall rapidly and the associated muscle will go weak. Conversely, if the energy flow to the meridian has not been disrupted, the muscle will test strong. This is not all.

A major discovery of Behavioral Kinesiology is that the thymus gland monitors and regulates energy flow in the meridian system.*

Think of the control room of a large electrical network. The dials in front represent the amount of energy flowing through each of the channels. Whenever an energy imbalance occurs, the controller takes immediate action to correct it. If the energy level is too high in a certain channel, he redirects it to channels where it is low; if the energy level is too low in a channel, he sends energy to it from higher-energy channels.

The controller of energy flow in the body is the thymus gland. Day after day, moment by moment, it monitors and rebalances our Life Energy. If it is not doing its job correctly and an imbalance develops, ultimately there will be physical damage to a particular organ. This is organic disease. At that point,

*This is the basis for instinctive behavior. But that is another story.

even if we can activate the thymus and get the energy flowing again, some structural weakness will remain. Thus the importance of primary prevention.

And so we have added another function to the "inactive" thymus gland.* The thymus, you may remember from Chapter 2, produces lymphocytes and later, through the release of hormones, controls them in such a way that foreign cells and substances and abnormal body cells are recognized and destroyed. This function, called immunological surveillance, is directly concerned with resistance to infection and cancer. It is only recently that the immunological functions of the thymus gland have been understood. Its role as master controller that directs the life-giving and the healing energies of the body has come as a complete surprise.

As we have seen, the thymus is the first organ of the body to be affected by stress. It is also the first organ to be affected at an energy level by an emotional state. The thymus gland may thus be thought of as the link between mind and body.

Interestingly enough, the word *thymus* is derived from the Greek *thymos*, or θυμός, which is untranslatable into modern terms but denoted life force, soul, and feeling or sensibility. As Onians† points out, *thymos* originally referred to the breath. It

---

*For a summary of the functions of the thymus gland, see Appendix I.

†Richard B. Onians, *The Origins of European Thought* (New York: Arno Press, 1973), pp. 44–65.

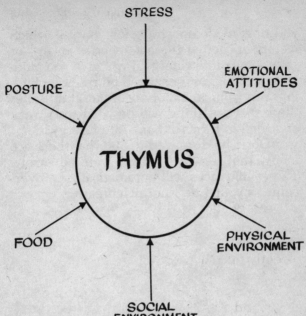

Fig. 12.

was the stuff of consciousness, the spirit, the breath-soul, upon which depended a man's energy and courage. Even the earliest origins of the word implied rising into flames, as a cloud, spirit, which relate it to the concept of soul and Life Energy.*

Besides being affected by stress and emotional states, the thymus is strongly influenced by an individual's physical environment, social relationships, food, and posture. These six major factors are summarized in Figure 12. In the rest of this book I will show

*For a fuller discussion of the word *thymos*, see Appendix II.

you how to demonstrate for yourself which factors in each of these categories lower—or raise—your Life Energy. I will give you guidance and suggestions based on research findings and clinical experience, but at all times the important thing will be what tests weak or strong in terms of *your* Life Energy.

Don't be dismayed to find that there are many things which affect you adversely. These influences will automatically be overcome as your Life Energy increases.

(5)

Stress and Cerebral Balance

"The personal issue is whether the things we are doing day by day are done in a conscious and balanced way or are part of a painridden struggle. If yours be the latter method, stop!"

—*Raymond A. Dart*

Test someone and find that the deltoid indicator muscle is strong. Now do anything to mildly shock him—jolt him, yell "BOO!" or anything similar. Test again. Suddenly that strong indicator muscle has gone weak.

I have demonstrated this on hundreds of people—doctors, patients, and the general public. Always the subject is amazed to find how susceptible he is to minor disturbances such as these. Perhaps the most astonished of all are doctors, especially when I use this simple example: In the doctor's presence I ask his receptionist to announce suddenly that a patient with whom the doctor is not very happy is calling him on the telephone, wanting to talk to him. Even though the doctor knows that this is only a demonstration, his receptionist's words—"Mr. Smith would like to talk to you"—trigger such a startle reaction that every muscle goes weak.

Repeat the experiment as above, but with this difference: Have your subject put his tongue against the roof of his mouth, the tip about a quarter of an inch behind the upper front teeth. In most instances you will find that the muscle now does not go weak, that your subject's energy is now intact.

What does this mean? When your subject is unaffected by these simple stress tests, he is what we call *centered*, or, better, his energies are centered and he is invulnerable to stress. To remain centered at all times is one of our primary goals. Let us use the following analogy: If a country is busy fighting small wars here and skirmishes there, there will be no troops available should they suddenly be needed against a major attack. Similarly, most of us function with our energies scattered throughout our bodies, with an inadequate supply in the energy reservoir. Hence, when we are confronted with the need for a sudden mobilization of energy, we have no reserves upon which to call. But if we are centered—if our Life Energy is at a high level and instantly available through the thymus gland—then when a sudden stress is introduced, immediate and appropriate action can be taken.

Many people are so uncentered that they are weakened by performing a simple task such as rubbing their nose or swinging a golf club. If you find such a subject, go one step further and have him simply *think* of carrying out one of these acts. Weakness in the indicator muscle will again be produced.

Take it even further. Have him say his name and address to himself. Just saying these (or any) words to himself diminishes his Life Energy so much that the muscle goes weak.

I sometimes encounter this phenomenon with people who practice meditation that involves the use of a mantra, or a silent saying. When an uncentered person recites the mantra, he is actually weakening himself. (Strangely enough, if he raises or lowers the pitch of his inner voice, he usually remains strong. But that is another story.)

What an indictment of our present lifestyle it is that so many people, just by hearing "BOO!" or saying their names and addresses to themselves, are so depleted of energy that all the muscles in their bodies go weak! Continual stress drains energy away from its seat, or home base, the thymus gland. But, as we have seen, there is a simple way to counteract the weakening effect of stress as it occurs. We can stimulate the thymus gland by thumping it or reflexly activate it by placing the tongue against the roof of the mouth with the tip on what we might call the "centering button."

During a tennis match, both players

tend to be weakened whenever the referee
makes a call. However, the player who has
his tongue on the centering button or whose
thymus has been otherwise activated will not
be affected by this call. Some very rewarding
results have been obtained with this centering technique in competitive sports activities.

It has been found that when the tongue
is on the centering button, the cerebral
hemispheres are balanced.

During the last decade or so, considerable research has been devoted to determining the specific functions of each hemisphere
of the brain. To summarize it briefly: In
right-handed people (in left-handers the results are not so consistent) the left cerebral
hemisphere seems to be involved primarily
in analytical thinking and verbal activity, and
the right hemisphere in intuitive and artistic
activities and orientation in space. The left
brain is thought to process information se-
quentially and the right brain, simultaneously.

Clues to the specialization of the two cerebral hemispheres came from surgical cases
in which the corpus callosum, the connection
between the hemispheres, was severed.
Clinical tests on these patients were interesting. If the subject was blindfolded and given
an object to hold in his right hand, he could
describe it verbally, but he could not do so if
the object was placed in his left hand. However, he could pick out the object he had

held in his left hand from a group of miscellaneous objects, showing that he recognized the object but could not talk about it. The explanation is this: The neural pathways from one side of the body cross over and go to the cerebral hemisphere on the opposite side. With the connections between the hemispheres severed, information about the object from nerve fibers in the left hand went to the right brain but did not get transferred to the left brain. Tests such as these confirmed what was learned from earlier studies—that the left hemisphere is the language center of the brain.

Let us now test for ourselves some of the separate functions of the hemispheres. This test, called the test for cerebral imbalance, is probably testing not only the cerebral cortex, but also associated areas beneath it.

Find a subject whose indicator muscle tests strong. Have him place the palm of his right hand approximately two to four inches off (away from) the left side of his head opposite the ear (see Figure 13). If he is balanced, his indicator muscle will stay strong (Figure 14); it will also remain strong when he places the palm of his right hand off the right side of his head opposite the ear (see Figures 15 and 16). This is as it should be. Having established this, give him a mathematical problem to try to do in his head, such as dividing 750 by 25. Immediately upon placing the palm of his right hand near the left side of his head, the indicator muscle will go weak, but this will not happen when he places the palm of

Fig. 13. Testing for cerebral balance. Position of hand when testing off the left hemisphere. Notice that the hand does not touch the head or the hair. Also, the palm of the hand must be in line with the ear and the head must be held straight.

Fig. 14. Actual testing off the left hemisphere.

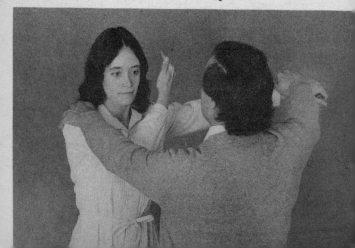

Fig. 15. Testing for cerebral balance. Position of hand when testing off the right hemisphere.

Fig. 16. Actual testing off the right hemisphere.

his right hand near the right side of his head. The opposite results will be obtained if you ask the subject to think of a musical tune. When the palm of his right hand is near the right side of his head, the indicator muscle will go weak, but not when the palm of his hand is near the left side. What we are testing is magnetic phenomena, not electroencephalographic activity.

Such testing can tell us a great deal about how a person handles stress. First let us consider the example of a telephone operator who is working under extreme pressure. There are two ways of dealing with this. One is to become even more methodical, even obsessional, and take care of each plug in turn while the calls are piling up and tension is increasing. This would be the left brain's answer. The right brain's answer would be to retreat into fantasy and figuratively "pull out all the plugs" until the tension has blown over.

Our findings corroborate this concept. People who characteristically test weak with the palm of the right hand *off* the left side of the head are left-hemisphere-dominant and tend to function under considerable nervous and emotional stress. In contrast, those who test weak *off* the right side of the head are right-hemisphere-dominant and tend to escape into fantasy and avoid unpleasant feelings.

But neither of these is a satisfactory solution. Throughout life we should never be so overcome by stress that either hemisphere should be dominant. Both hemispheres should be working together at all times. However, we rarely find this. Most people will test weak on the left side, showing left-hemisphere dominance, which means that they are trying to cope under too much stress. They are caught in a verbal, intellectual struggle with the environment, greatly impoverished because they have lost the aesthetic and intuitive aspects of their existence, the right-hemisphere contribution.

It is not only desirable, it is normal that the two hemispheres are working together throughout the waking day; that when we talk, there is a rhythm and a cadence to our voices; that when we walk, there is a flow and a grace to our movements; that when we think, the logic of our thoughts does not shut out intuition and spatial perception. When both hemispheres are fully active and integrated with each other, this is the condition of *creativity*, man's highest functioning. Unfortunately, this does not occur very often. In fact, it occurs so infrequently that patients in whom the two hemispheres have been surgically separated cannot be easily distinguished from other people, because in "normal" people the hemispheres aren't working together either!

So Behavioral Kinesiology has given us an easy way of determining which hemisphere tends to be dominant, suggesting patterns of an individual's response to stress. Has stress driven him into extreme left-brain-hemisphere, obsessional, intellectual activity, or has it driven him into extreme right-brain-hemisphere, escapist activity? Neither of these is as it should be. Everyone should be functioning with both hemispheres at all times. If a person who is strongly centered is presented with a mathematical problem, the two hemispheres will remain balanced, and the beauty and, in certain cases, the elegance of the mathematical solution will come into play.

Well, we may ask, it may be ideal to have the two hemispheres balanced and working together, but how can we achieve this under the day-to-day stresses and pressures of life?

Enter the thymus gland again. Whenever there is an asymmetry in the working of the two hemispheres, thymus activity will be impaired. Fortunately, this phenomenon works the other way as well—if the thymus is stimulated, the two hemispheres will also tend to be balanced. Therefore, all the factors mentioned throughout this book that will increase thymus activity (the *thymos*), and hence the Life Energy, will at the same time keep the two cerebral hemispheres working together, making us creative, enabling us to experience life in the whole, and furthermore, reducing tension and stress. Stress patterns are self-defeating, for when stress forces us to work, as it were, with just one hemisphere, it becomes much harder to be creative and solve the problem and hence reduce the stress. Two hemispheres are better than one!

Demonstrate for yourself the effect of activating the thymus on someone who tests weak off one side of the head. The easiest method is to thump the thymus several times. Test again. You will probably find that the two hemispheres are balanced. But there is a way in which this can be enhanced.

There are certain activities that appear to be mainly verbal and left-hemisphere-dominant, but really are dual-hemisphere— that is, they require the functioning of both cerebral hemispheres. One of these is the reading of poetry. Again, test this for yourself.

Find someone who tests weak off the left side of the head and get him to read aloud a piece of ordinary newspaper prose. He will usually still test weak. The hemispheres have not been balanced by this activity. One is still dominant. Now give your subject a poem and have him read it in an ordinary, unrhythmic fashion, as if he were reading the newspaper. Again the two hemispheres will not be balanced. Now have him read the poem in a very rhythmic fashion. (This is very effective with poetry that has a strong basic rhythm as do many of the poems of W. B. Yeats, particularly the earlier ones.) Test again. You will find that both hemispheres are balanced! The reading of poetry is clearly a dual-hemisphere activity, combining the verbal skills of the left hemisphere that are involved in all reading with the musical and rhythmical qualities controlled by the right hemisphere. (Strangely enough, the results are not usually as dramatic with singing, and this I cannot explain.)

Another activity that tends to balance the hemispheres is looking at landscape paintings, particularly the works of Turner. The results are not nearly so satisfactory with line drawings or with photographs. Looking at a beautiful scene in nature may or may not be as effective, depending on the ability of the viewer to abstract certain qualities from it, which is, after all, what a good painter has already done for us.

I have found that if people take an "energy break" every so often—just to recite a verse or two of poetry or to look at a picture postcard of a painting, stress and tension will be considerably reduced. The thymus will test strong, and the Life Energy will be high. The results are enhanced if the thymus is tapped at the same time. Try it!

A common activity that leads to hemisphere imbalance is listening on the telephone. If you hold the receiver to your left ear, you will find that during your telephone conversation and for a short time after, you will test weak if the palm of your right hand is held off the left side of your head. Apparently, listening with the left ear has encouraged left-hemisphere-dominant activity. Conversely, if the receiver is held to the right ear, right-hemisphere activity will prevail. The remedy for this, of course, is to alternate the ear with which you listen. You can also tap the thymus from time to time or take an energy break.

Switching is a term coined by Goodheart to describe a state in which there is a particular type of body confusion. In Behavioral Kinesiology, switching has been found to be a distinct manifestation of cerebral-hemisphere imbalance.

Try the following demonstration. Have a subject read any prose passage forward. Then stop his reading and immediately test him in the clear. Most likely, his indicator muscle will test weak. Now have him read the passage backward, word by word. Test him again. He will not test weak! The asymmetry between the two cerebral hemispheres has produced a bizarre type of dyslexia (subtle reading disability). Now, if this asymmetry is producing *this* imbalance, as indicated by your subject's muscle weakness, then it must also be causing other subtle but not insignificant perceptual difficulties. And these subtle perceptual difficulties, often leading to a vague feeling of confusion, have been reported time after time.

It was Carl Delacato* who first noted that in many children with neurological problems, particularly those involved with speech and reading, there was a regression to or fixation at an early stage of locomotion and hence of neurological organization. When a baby first begins to crawl, he crawls in what is called a homolateral fashion—he uses his left arm and leg (and right arm and

*Carl H. Delacato, Ed.D. *The Diagnosis and Treatment of Speech and Reading Problems* (Springfield: Charles C. Thomas, 1963).

leg) at the same time, as a lizard does and as
trotting pacer horses are trained to do. However, as the baby achieves a higher level of
neurological integration, he adopts a cross-
crawl pattern—opposite arms and legs—the
pattern of our normal walk. Now, when a
person is "switched," he tends to revert to
the homolateral level of locomotion. If asked
to march off briskly, he is likely to swing the
same arm and leg. This homolateral gait can
switch a person easily. Try it yourself with a
subject whose hemispheres prove to be balanced, and whose indicator muscle in the
clear and thymus gland point test strong
when he reads forward or backward. Tell
him to march with his left arm forward when
his left leg is forward, and vice versa. Test
again. You will find that the thymus now
tests weak, the two cerebral hemispheres are
unbalanced, and, furthermore, when he
reads *forward*, his indicator muscle will go
weak! A primitive pattern of neurological organization has taken over from the more mature pattern present only a minute before!

People who are under constant stress
may function with this switching pattern as
their "normal" mode of behavior. One of the
standard procedures in treatment is to teach
them to do heterolateral walking and crawl-
ing (opposite arm and leg forward). This exercise, along with the reciting of poetry in a
rhythmic fashion, the viewing of landscape
paintings, enhanced by thumping the thymus, should correct most imbalances between the two hemispheres and correct all
switching tendencies.

However, there are many day-to-day activities that cause us to switch and therefore to become neurologically disorganized. These activities may also create barely noticeable patterns of cerebral confusion that lead to increased stress, thus compounding the whole situation. Here are a few examples.

Physical exercises involving the use of both arms and/or legs at the same time, or of the left arm and leg or the right arm and leg simultaneously, will cause switching. The most obvious of these is old-fashioned jumping jacks. Even *thinking* about doing jumping jacks will make you switch, showing that switching is due to brain patterns rather than feed-back from the muscles. Other common exercises that lead to cerebral imbalance are weight-pulling, weight-lifting, and rowing motions. So stick to exercises that use opposite arms and legs, or just one arm at a time. Vigorous walking with the right arm forward when the left leg is forward and vice versa is one of the best. By doing such exercises you are truly strengthening yourself, which, after all, is the purpose of exercise. If you usually operate under stress and have a tendency to switch, just thinking about walking as you swing opposite arms and legs will help you considerably.

Bicycling will also cause you to switch. Whenever you ride a bicycle, give your thymus a few thumps from time to time.

Have you ever wondered why nearly all tennis players find the backhand so much more difficult than the forehand? One rea-

son is that when performing a backhand
stroke the player is likely to switch. Remember the difference between homolateral and
heterolateral gaits (p. 78). A forehand tennis
swing involves primarily a movement forward of both the left leg and the right arm—
in essence, heterolateral gait, which is normal. But the backhand involves primarily a
forward movement of the right leg and the
right arm—in essence, a homolateral gait.
And this causes switching. A tennis player
can reduce the tendency to switch by using
the various techniques presented in this and
other chapters.

A related point is that tennis is a game in
which you use both legs but only one arm. If
you are right-handed, your left arm is relatively inactive, which tends to cause a cerebral imbalance with the left hemisphere
dominant—that is, stress and switching problems. (The right arm, of course, activates the
left hemisphere.) The solution is to transfer
your racquet to your left hand at the end of
each rally and make a few strokes with it to
activate your right hemisphere and hence re-
balance and center yourself.

Poor posture, to which I devote a chapter, can also lead to cerebral imbalance.
However, body movements and positions are
not the only causes of this problem. Metal
crossing the middle of the body, particularly
in the head and neck region where the energy channels (meridians) are more "concentrated," tends to cause switching, although
not if the metal makes a full circle as in the

case of a necklace. People who have metal partial dentures that cross the midline may complain of feeling confused and somewhat irritable. They say that they are thinking less clearly than they once did. When the metal dental appliance is altered so that it no longer crosses the midline, these people report tremendous improvement, and no longer test as being switched. One woman said that for the first time in fifteen years, since she had her partial fitted, she awakens in the morning and knows exactly where she is. Previously it had taken her some minutes to sort out her thoughts and to collect herself.

The switching effect of metal crossing the body's midline is not noticed with belt buckles, because the energy channels are widely separated at the waist. But switching is certainly induced by metal-framed spectacles. It is ironic that reading difficulties can be compounded by the very devices used to overcome them. The single expedient of changing from metal-framed to plastic-framed glasses has made a considerable difference to many patients.

Being uncentered, having a general cerebral hemisphere imbalance, and being switched are related manifestations of stress that lead to a reduction of the Life Energy. In this chapter I have offered you some simple techniques to counteract these conditions. Get in the habit of taking an energy break several times a day. Read a few verses of a favorite poem and enjoy a postcard-size reproduction of a painting that you can put in your pocket. Take a walk with arms swinging freely. If you feel stress building up, check your tongue position and thump your thymus. Your body will respond to these activities immediately. Other techniques for reducing stress will be suggested throughout this book as we discuss other aspects of the environment that may affect your Life Energy.

(6)

Your Emotions and Your Thymus

"Enlightened love is the universal medicine."

—*Manly P. Hall*

I have said that the thymus gland is the first organ to be affected at an energy level by an emotional state. This effect is instantaneous and easy to demonstrate. Find a person whose thymus point tests weak and have him think of someone he loves, or of something pleasant, such as lying in the sun on the beach. Whatever it is, the image strengthens the thymus at once. Now ask the person to think of someone he hates, or of something unpleasant, such as being ill. The thymus will return to its weak state.

So here's another activity to add to your energy break or to carry out whenever you are frightened, upset, or under stress. Find out what thought is most effective in strengthening your thymus. This is your *homing* thought. Come back to it often.

Unfortunately, 95 percent of the people I have tested have an underactive thymus gland. This means that most of us are involved too much with unpleasantnesses and hate-provoking situations and not nearly enough with pleasant and loving situations. Too many problems, not enough lying on the beach. Too many people we hate; not enough people we love.

A young male patient who had been given a diagnosis of cancer came to me for holistic therapy. In the course of the interview I asked him, "Do you hate anyone?" He said, "I loathe and detest my mother." When he test-touched his thymus, it was weak. I said, "As long as you hate your mother, this hatred will so diminish your thymus activity, your Life Energy, that you will never get completely well." He said, "I would sooner die than give up hating my mother." And that was the end of the session!

The emotional states that weaken the thymus are hate, envy, suspicion, and fear. Their opposites, which activate the thymus, are benevolent love, faith, trust, courage, and gratitude. These positive feelings are the deepest and most beautiful emotions there are.

While no one can have positive thoughts and attitudes all of the time, everyone can have them most of the time. It is largely a matter of *will*. The role of the will is easily overlooked in present-day psychiatry. I believe that we are ruled by our subconscious if only we *choose to be*. Once we have been convinced by BK testing that hateful and destructive thoughts can deplete our Life Energy (*thymos*) and that loving and nurturing thoughts can increase it, the decision is ours as to which path to take. Now, I'm not suggesting that we suppress our negative thoughts; rather that we turn them into positive ones. This, of course, is difficult, but it should be our ideal, and BK testing confirms that such transformations are indeed beneficial to thymus activity. It is a matter of changing our attitudes. We are doing this for our own benefit as well as for others. It is as much to our advantage to love as to be loved. If we respond to others with hatred, our Life Energy will be diminished; if we respond with love, it will be raised. Test this for yourself. It is not easy to change hateful feelings into loving ones, but it is one of the steps to positive health.

This whole matter of negative emotions has far-reaching implications. Now, it is an axiom of most of the popular psychologies of the day, and of modern psychiatry as well, that we should "let it all hang out"—that we should openly express what we feel. The idea is that if the psychopathological "pus" inside us is squeezed and released, we will be cured. I'll never forget a schizophrenic patient of mine who at the end of his first therapy session walked to the door and very po-

litely said, "Thank you, Doctor." He then
dropped his trousers and defecated on my
carpet, again thanked me, closed the door,
and left. Now, this is *not*, in my opinion, what
psychotherapy is about. Psychotherapy is not
to help the patient get his negative emotions
out, but to help him turn them into positive
ones.

As an example, let's take the case of a
young married woman who had been a patient of mine for about six months. When she
started therapy, she had an underactive thymus and another problem—her heart meridian continually tested weak. Now, I have
found that this meridian is usually associated
with the emotion of anger. This particular
patient was having marital difficulties and
was often very angry with her husband;
hence the persistent energy imbalance in the
heart meridian. With therapy and thymus
supplements, her thymus gland had been
consistently strong for some time. But she
was still having trouble with the heart meridian. One day she came in and said, "Doctor, I
feel so pleased with myself. For the first time
last night I was able to express my anger to
my husband." She test-touched her heart
meridian test point (located one-half to one
inch below the point where the lower ribs
meet). We found it strong. *But*, upon testing
the thymus gland, we found that it was weak!

She tapped her thymus several times
(see page 50) and it tested strong. Then I said
to her, "Think of feeling angry with your
husband." We tested again and now her

heart meridian was weak! Next I said to her, "Think about really letting it out, really expressing your anger like you did last night." I tested her thymus again. It was weak! Her heart meridian tested strong, but even the thought of lashing out at her husband had caused her thymus to go into a negative energy imbalance, in spite of the therapy and the thymus supplements. She was now worse than before. She had gone from a localized imbalance of meridian energy to a generalized imbalance of total body energy. She said, "I understand what has happened. But what do I do now?" I said, "Concentrate on turning your anger into forgiveness and understanding and love. Recognize that there may be many things that your husband does that you don't like, but that you love him as a person." After she made this change in her underlying attitude, her thymus and heart points tested strong. And since that time there has been a great improvement in her marriage.

If you're not convinced that psychotherapy as commonly practiced is debilitating, try this: Have your thymus tested by the test-touch technique. It should be strong. If it is weak, temporarily activate it by tapping lightly two or three times. Now start to talk to someone as if he were your psychiatrist. Tell him about the difficulties you are having with your spouse, the hard time your boss is giving you, and so forth. Test again. Instantly your thymus gland has been weakened. Just think—you can spend years in therapy, and session after session your thymus gland is being weakened because you are continually dwelling on the negative. You may come out of therapy with a better understanding of your problems, but the end result will be a diminution of your Life Energy.

But, you say, isn't that what psychotherapy should be—discussing what's wrong so that it can be relieved? Yes, of course, by all means mention what is wrong, but not to have it discussed and analyzed and "worked through." Bring up your negative emotions and change them into positive ones instantly, then and there. If you do, you will leave the sessions with a lighter step, with a smile on your face. And spare a kind thought for your therapist. The more you concentrate on positive emotions, the less he'll suffer—because if he is sympathetic, he will probably be affected to some degree by your energy imbalances. More about this in Chapter 7.

There is another way of controlling our emotional states besides changing our attitudes, and that is through our gestures and facial expressions. Two of the most universal of all gestures are the vertical nodding of the head for acceptance and the shaking of the head from side to side for rejection. Now, all gestures relate to specific meridians; these gestures of acceptance and rejection relate directly to the thymus, the monitoring center for energy imbalances of the entire meridian system.

This can be easily demonstrated. Ask someone whose thymus tests weak to nod his head several times. The thymus will now test strong. Conversely, ask someone whose thymus tests strong to shake his head from side to side. His thymus will test weak.

The most powerful gesture of love is the outstretching of arms to embrace. This "Madonna" gesture, made toward a frightened child or someone who is troubled, will instantly strengthen the weak thymus. It will also benefit the person who is in this manner offering his or her love. Thus, whenever you're under stress, make the thymus gesture, as I call it, or imagine yourself doing so. In either case, think of the outflow of love that goes with it.

We have always known how beautiful and beneficial a smile is. Now we can show—actually demonstrate—the therapeutic value of smiling. The smile muscle is called the zygomaticus major. However, a true smile also involves the muscles of the lower eyelid; otherwise it is a cold smile, the "gambler's smile." While the other muscles of the body are associated with specific meridians, the zygomaticus major is linked to the thymus gland.

If you find someone who is weak on test-touching the thymus point, have him smile. He will test strong. The same strengthening effect will be obtained if, instead of having him smile, you tweak his cheeks as you would a baby's. Receptors in the skin over the smile muscle seem to activate this mechanism. You have tricked the subject's body into thinking that he has smiled.

Fig. 17. The "Madonna," or thymus, gesture. Murillo, "The Vision of St. Felix of Cantalicio."

Fig. 18. The thymus gesture.

Fig. 19. Another example of the thymus gesture—reaching out with love. Vincent Van Gogh, "The First Steps."

But now tweak another set of points, those at the sides of the chin where frequently, in sad people, the corners turn down. You are tricking the subject's sensors into believing that he looks sad and feels sad—that he is literally "down at the mouth." Not only the subject, but you, the tester, and any onlookers as well will test weak for the thymus point. These "up buttons" and "down buttons" (the heavy dots on the diagrams) affect not only the people "pushing" them but also anyone looking at them.

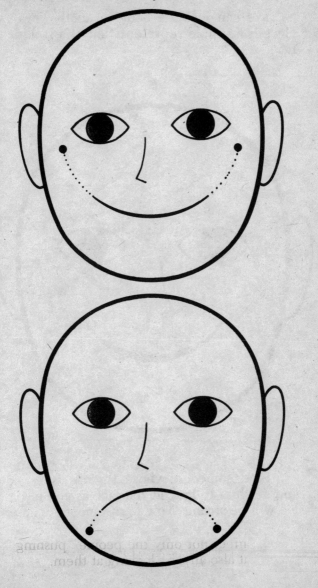

We can fool the body in another way. Here is a simple representation of a smiling face.

Find someone whose thymus is weak and get him to look at the face as you test.* He will be strong. Now find someone whose

*When testing one of two or more figures or pictures appearing on the same page, cover the ones not being tested.

thymus is strong and have him look at this representation of a sad face. His thymus will test weak.

We can abstract this still further. Just have the subject look at a line going up or a line going down. The test results will be the same.

These symbols are innate. They are what we use all the time to assess everyone with whom we come in contact. We ask ourselves: Do they like me? Do they dislike me? Are they sad? Are they happy? We judge, and we are judged, by such subtle clues.

Have a look at the two drawings below. Looking at the top one will not weaken your Life Energy, but looking at the bottom one will. What is the difference?

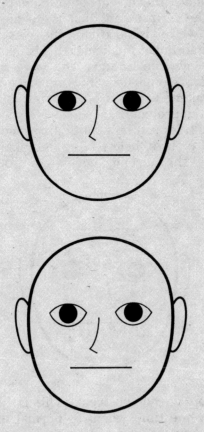

*For a discussion of sanpaku eyes, see *You Are All Sanpaku* by George Oshawa, English version by William Dufty (Secaucus, N.J.: University Books, 1965).

The bottom pictures shows *sanpaku* eyes,* which are a characteristic of many famous people, including John F. Kennedy, Abraham Lincoln, and Marilyn Monroe. *San* in Japanese means three, and *paku*, sides. Thus, the term means that there are three sides of white visible around the eyes. In Japanese traditional medicine, this is taken as a sign of low Life Energy. And in fact, when we look at someone with sanpaku eyes, we are weakened, unless our thymus is strong enough to protect us.

Consider just how subtle these clues are. A third picture, below, shows sanpaku eyes, as does the second, but when you look

at it you do not go weak. This is because there is one time when it's normal to have white showing under the eye, and that's when we're looking up. The third picture suggests that the person is looking up, because there are wrinkles on the forehead.

Thus, you respond in the second picture to someone with weak energy, but in the third one you say in effect, "This person does not have weak energy. He is just a normal-appearing person looking up." Such responses demonstrate that even these little line drawings are potent symbols that can give us incredibly different messages.

If you have sanpaku eyes, you need to strengthen your thymus gland and thereby increase your Life Energy. Frequent smiling is one of the best ways to do this. Unfortunately, many people report that it is *hard* for them to smile. They say it's as if their smile muscles have to be "cranked up." Now, we know that when we reach early middle age, our facial muscles begin to sag. This is more pronounced in some people; it really is mechanically difficult for them to smile. Moreover, as they grow older, they may feel that there is nothing to smile about. We may then ask, do we feel like smiling when our facial structure makes it easy for us to smile, or does feeling like smiling facilitate the physical act of smiling? I suspect it is a circular process. Whatever the case, if we cannot smile readily and easily, we are lacking an important mechanism for continually activating the thymus and thereby tonifying our bodies. A smile wipes the blackboard clean.

To demonstrate the debilitating effect of slack facial muscles, find someone whose thymus tests strong and have him assume a "hang-dog" look by letting all his facial mus-

Fig. 20. Notice Lincoln's sanpaku eyes.

cles droop. His thymus will then test weak. However, even with the "hang-dog" look, if he places the tip of his tongue on the centering button, this negative effect on the thymus gland will be abolished. This shows the supreme importance of keeping our tongues in this position at all times. This is the *normal* position for the tongue. In this position the entire body is tonified through the relationship between the centering button and the body energy system and of course the Life Energy.

Now, people who have inadequate development of the palatal arch—the arch that contains the upper teeth—have facial muscles that hang loose and flabby. There are two reasons for faulty palatal arch development. One is incorrect bottle feeding (and frequently incorrect breast feeding) in which the tongue is forced down to the floor of the mouth. In its normal position at the roof of the mouth, the tongue is constantly providing a pressure, heightened by swallowing, that is necessary for the forward and lateral development of the arch. This expansion does not take place when the tongue is resting loosely on the floor of the mouth.

The other cause of faulty arch development is maternal malnutrition. In the 1930s and 1940s a dentist by the name of Weston Price studied many "primitive" races throughout the world. He found that whenever the people changed from their usual diets to a "modern" diet of imported foods— white flour, refined sugar, polished rice, and

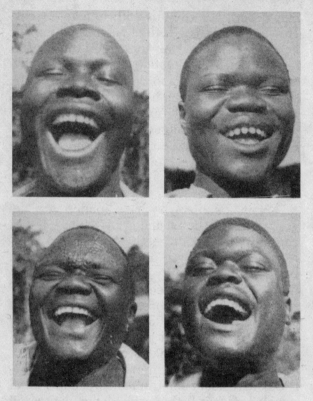

Fig. 21. An example of the wide palatal arches of "primitive" people.

the like—there was *in the same generation* an outbreak of dental decay previously unknown. Furthermore, he found that *within one generation* the size of the palatal arch and the mandible was greatly reduced.*

*Weston A. Price, *Nutrition and Physical Degeneration: A Comparison of Primitive and Modern Diets and Their Effects* (Santa Monica, Calif.: 1945, 1970). Price-Pottenger Nutrition Foundation.

Now, the palatal arch forms at eight and a half weeks of intra-uterine life, when the fetus is only an inch or so long. If the mother is inadequately nourished at this time, the arch will tend to be high and narrow rather than broad and fully developed. This faulty development of the palatal arch is one of the dearest prices we have paid for our "civilization." It is hard for most of us to smile. Now, I'm not saying that a narrow face in itself precludes an easy smile; the palatal arch may be in the correct proportion to the rest of the skull and provide adequate stretch for the smile muscle. What I'm saying is that a narrow face, especially in the lower portion, suggests a faulty palatal arch. When we look at the pictures in Weston Price's book, we see people with faces so broad they seem to be smiling all the time (see Figure 21).

Let us examine this facial-structure problem another way.

Find someone whose thymus is weak. Put a roll of cotton wool between the upper teeth and the cheek on each side and test the thymus again. It will be strong. Stretching of the smile muscle was all that was needed to correct multiple energy problems throughout the body. A number of dental appliances have been developed that have the same effect as the cotton wool. Used in this way, they have been found to be highly beneficial.

Can the palatal arch be expanded mechanically? This is very difficult in adults. In children it is a fairly easy orthodontic procedure, and much more effective than the usual ones.

I have often stated in lectures that one of the greatest gifts a mother can give her un-born child is a well-formed palatal arch so that the smile muscles will be in proper tension. It will be easy for such a child to smile as he goes through life. And every time he smiles he will be balancing and correcting all the energy problems in his body, and thus raising his Life Energy. The easier it is for him to smile, the more he will smile, the more he will feel like smiling, the happier he will be, and the happier he will make people around him.

So smile. Think of things to make you smile, and if you can't, or if you don't feel like smiling at the moment, you can always tweak your "up button."

(7)

The People
Around You

"We have lost the art of living; and in the most important science of all, the science of daily life, the science of behavior, we are complete ignoramuses!"

—*D. H. Lawrence*

We are much more easily influenced by people around us than we realize. Let's make a simple test.

Take two people, one whose thymus tests strong and one whose thymus tests weak. Have them sit side by side, paying no particular attention to one another. Test their thymus glands in this situation and it will be as before—one will be strong and the other will be weak. Now have them face each other and ask them to get involved, either by talking or by looking closely at each other. Retest. You will almost always find that the person whose thymus was strong is now testing weak, and often but not invariably that the person whose thymus was weak is now testing strong. Somehow the Life Energy of the "strong" person was diminished by his coming into personal contact with someone with a weak thymus. Not only this: If you test various meridian (energy system) test points throughout the bodies of the interacting subjects, you will find that a specific imbalance can be transmitted from one person to another.

This phenomenon, which is the basis of sympathy (literally, same feeling), occurs throughout our lives, whenever we become involved in some way with another person. Doctors, dentists, nurses, psychotherapists, social workers, the clergy—anyone who administers to the ill or the troubled—are particularly vulnerable. I have tested hundreds of doctors and have found that 85 to 90 percent of these caring and sympathetic practitioners of the healing arts suffer from underactive thymus glands.

What does this all mean? Should Life Energy be a consideration when we choose our friends and associates? And our sleeping partners? And, of course, our husbands and wives?

We could, of course, go through life avoiding personal involvement with other people, detaching ourselves, protecting ourselves by closing down communications. But this is not desirable, this is not natural. It may protect us, but it will greatly impoverish us, and others as well.

The answer is to raise our Life Energy sufficiently so that we are unaffected. We can then become involved and sympathetic, but not be weakened in the process. If our Life Energy is high, others will benefit from close contact with us; if it is low, our relationships with others become part of the general problem. This leads to what I regard as the basis of all ethical behavior—the *reciprocal thymus relationship*. If we raise our Life Energy, we are raising that of every member of our family; if those close to us raise their Life Energy, ours will be increased.

Should we not also expect high Life Energy of our schoolteachers, our pilots, our political leaders? On these people our well-being, our very lives may depend.

If you have any doubts about the ease with which we are affected by other people, consider what happens in surrogate testing. Goodheart showed many years ago that if the test subject was unable to cooperate—for example, if he was too young or was unconscious—then the testing could be carried out using a surrogate, preferably the mother or spouse, but anybody with whom personal involvement could be established. If you want to test someone's thymus using a surrogate, have a person who tests strong test-touch the subject's thymus while the two are in close physical contact. Then test the surrogate. If the surrogate now goes weak, it means that the subject's thymus is underactive. It also means that there is something wrong with the surrogate's thymus, although this may only be revealed at deeper levels of testing. Because the surrogate can be affected by someone else as easily as this, he is quite vulnerable to the reciprocal thymus relationship.

One particular characteristic of a person to which we respond strongly is his or her voice. As we will discuss in Chapter 9, the sounds of nature can be therapeutic. So can the human voice, *your* voice.

Find someone whose thymus is weak and talk to him as you test him. Say something; if you wish, just count. The content of what you say is not important. If your voice is therapeutic, you will somehow have raised his Life Energy, rebalanced his energy systems, and corrected his underactive thymus. If it is not, you yourself are at the moment in a state of stress that is picked up by your subject. In the latter case, reduce your stress as I have suggested—for example, by reciting poetry and thumping the thymus (see Chapter 5 on stress). Then test the person again. You should now find that as you count he will test strong—that your voice has corrected his energy imbalance!

The voices of all of us are therapeutic if our hemispheres are balanced, if our own Life Energy is high when we are speaking, and if, deep down, our intent, out of love or concern, is to strengthen. Listen to the people around you. Listen to your TV and radio announcers. Listen to your leaders. Listen to your psychotherapist. Are their voices therapeutic or not? Are they in a state of stress when they are talking?

When you were a child, you may have retorted to a playmate that "Sticks and stones can break my bones, but names can never hurt me." This is just not true. Find someone whose thymus is strong and say to him, "You are ugly," or "I hate you." His indicator muscle will go weak, either in the clear or on test-touching the thymus.

Now turn this around the other way. Find someone whose thymus tests weak and say to him, "I love you." His thymus will test strong. We are only beginning to learn through Behavioral Kinesiology of the tremendous power of words, either to help or to harm others.

When we speak while we're not under stress, the two hemispheres of the brain are working together—the left providing the logic and the communication, the right adding the rhythmic and intuitive aspects of our delivery.

To demonstrate this, find a subject whose thymus gland is weak and have someone speak to him—even count—while you're testing. If the speaker has an active thymus—that is, if his stress pattern is relatively low—then his voice will "fix" the thymus of the other person. If, however, he is under stress, his voice will not be therapeutic.

I have found that when there is an imbalance between the cerebral hemispheres on testing there will also be an imbalance on testing of the muscles attached to the hyoid bone. This is a small bone in the neck to which all the muscles of speech are attached directly and indirectly. It seems that when we talk under stress our speech is subtly distorted by this hyoid imbalance. This distortion is picked up albeit unconsciously by the listener. It may also be picked up by sophisticated electronic "lie detection" equipment. However, such apparatus is not necessary. BK testing will work just as well.

Corroborative proof is that if we deliberately create an imbalance of the muscles attached to the hyoid we introduce an imbalance of the cerebral hemispheres. I have prepared a demonstration tape of the identical words being spoken by the same subject as I alternately introduce and then correct a hyoid imbalance. When I play this tape, the voice has a corresponding weakening and strengthening effect on the listener.

Although there's no way that we can find out by BK testing if someone is lying, we can certainly determine whether someone is under stress while speaking. I have done this hundreds of times, with results that correlate closely with those obtained by a lie detector.

As an example, there is a tape of my own voice that does not strengthen anyone. This recording was made shortly after my return to bed following a minor surgical procedure, performed under local anesthesia. In this tape I state how well I feel, but my voice fools no one. No one's thymus has ever been strengthened by that voice.

Consider these examples from recent political history:

- When Chief Justice Earl Warren is swearing in Richard Nixon for his first term in the Presidency, Warren says: "Do you, Richard Milhous Nixon ..." and his voice tests strong. But when Nixon himself repeats the oath, his voice tests weak, a pattern found throughout his entire inaugural speech.
- Harry S. Truman's voice almost invariably has a strengthening effect, except when he states that he is not running for reelection.
- Lyndon B. Johnson's voice does not strengthen when he says we are under attack by enemy forces in the Gulf of Tonkin, a statement which was not true.
- The voice of Senator Edward M. Kennedy does not have a positive effect when he talks about Chappaquiddick, because he must certainly be under a great deal of stress at the time he is speaking.

Perhaps the most pathetic example of vocal stress is the voice of Dr. Phillip Blaiberg, who was at the time the longest-surviving heart-transplant patient, saying how healthy and happy he feels. But this could not have been the case, as his voice was just not therapeutic. And he died shortly after that recording was made.

This stress-detection test is easy to carry out. It can be conducted while listening to the person live or from a tape recording of the voice. The voice may tell some, but the thymus tells all.

Remember, though, we're not testing for lying, we're only testing the degree of stress in the voice. For this to have validity we need to test in ten layers, only one of which we are talking about in this book, so please be prudent in your use of this information.

To be weakened by another person, you need not be face to face or even one to one.

Your involvement can, for example, be over television. I have found by BK testing that certain qualities of our charismatic leaders and television personalities can be transmitted in this way. If a public figure has a specific energy (meridian) imbalance or an underactive thymus, he can adversely affect a large number of people. An emotional state, negative or positive, can spread through a community and even a country from its primary source, the television personality, to the viewers, to their neighbors, and to all the people with whom they come in contact. If we are susceptible—of low Life Energy—we can pick up like an infection the emotional attitudes that are "going around."

Before the Industrial Revolution, when even what is now New York City was largely farmland, most people lived in villages. They knew the folks in the village itself, those who visited the village, and perhaps some friends whom they visited in the surrounding area. In his entire lifetime an individual might come in contact with only a few thousand people.

Nowadays we may make contact with that many people in a given day. If we live in a large city, there may be several hundred people in our apartment building alone. Each day on television, on the radio, and in newspapers we are exposed to thousands of people, few of whom are on a positive-energy course. And because so much news reporting is devoted to murders, assassinations, hijackings, floods, fires, and other disasters, we are bound to be adversely affected. Every act of violence on television, of which there are about a thousand a week, will weaken our thymus gland and our Life Energy.

Not only are we confronted in the media with pictures of terrorists, arsonists, child molesters, and other weakening people of our time, we are also sometimes treated to the likes of Adolf Hitler, a figure nearly as menacing in death as he was in life. (Just look at a photo of him and see how it destroys your thymus.)

Take a newspaper or a news magazine and determine how many photographs will cause your thymus to test weak. In a typical issue there will be many. It is just not possible to look at a news photograph of an assassination, or of a mutilated body, or of a traffic accident, without your thymus gland testing weak and your Life Energy being reduced. And this is happening day after day to millions of people.

Advertisements, too, can weaken you, particularly closeup photos of people smoking cigarettes. Before you can shift your eyes from the billboard or turn the page of the magazine, the message has registered. You have picked up certain minimal visual clues without being aware of it.

Portrait paintings have a powerful effect on us, too.* For example, consider a painting by Velázquez that cost the Metropolitan Museum of Art over five million dollars. Looking at this portrait of Juan de Pareja makes nearly everyone weak. Test for yourself (see Figure 22). Another portrait on view at the same museum makes everyone strong on testing. This is Rembrandt's Christ (see Figure 23).

Why do we go weak when we look at the Velázquez painting? I do not know. If you look at another artist's version (Figure 24), you will most likely test strong! The differences between the authentic picture and the copy are slight, yet the body evidently picks them up.

In Figures 25 and 26 are two very popular posters of the famous actress and model Farrah Fawcett-Majors. Contrast the effect of each on your Life Energy by having someone test you. If you respond as most people do, Figure 25 will not weaken you, but Figure 26 will. Obviously, there is nothing "wrong" with Farrah that makes you weak; there is just some part of her expression in the poster shown in Figure 26 that is affecting your thymus. Yet millions have been sold.

*For a discussion of symbols in paintings, see p. 139.

Fig. 22. "Portrait of Juan de Pareja" by Diego Rodriguez de Silva y Velázquez.

Fig. 23. Rembrandt's "Head of Christ."

Fig. 24. Artist's copy of Velázquez's portrait of Juan de Pareja.

Fig. 25. Poster of Farrah Fawcett-Majors. How does she affect you?

What does this tell us about the taste of the males of today?

Do you want to find which part of her expression causes the weakness? Just cover the mouth and have someone test you again.

Let us think for a moment about the nature of photographs.

Photography is a comparatively recent invention and has taken the place of drawing and painting for recording a scene or captur-

Fig. 26. One of the most popular posters of all time.

ing a person's likeness. But drawings and paintings, even those that are representational, are abstractions. The artist chooses certain aspects of the real world to highlight or to show in relation to other elements of his picture. Thus, he can soften a scene of destruction or transcend the horror of a subject. Now, some great journalistic photography can do this. Such photography is an art form as much as is painting. But the average journalism type of photography shows us the naked and unadorned reality of a situation, sometimes so starkly that most people cannot deal with it.

The terrible fascination such photographs hold for us binds us to them as personal attraction binds us to one another. In both cases, meridian (energy system) imbalances are introduced. They may be invoked by the harsh reality of the photo or acquired by transference from the imbalances of the people caught by the camera. Similarly, the manipulative photography of the advertising world, with its distortion and exaggeration and its ability to fascinate, leads to imbalances in the viewer.

In this chapter I have concentrated on the negative effects of our social environment. However, if news photographs show us a fireman holding a child he has just rescued, or if we see an inspiring, vital person on television, we are made richer in Life Energy. Unfortunately, people and the media being what they are, the negative influences greatly outweigh the positive ones. When you consider the cumulative effect, it is not surprising that we are living in a low-energy, thymus-weakening society.

(8)

Your Physical Environment

"Most wholesome physic of thy health-giving air."

—Shakespeare

We live in a time of great technological innovation. Every innovation modifies to some degree the patterns of living that have been established over millennia. We are actually experimental subjects, and the results are not yet in!

For many years I have used BK to investigate the environments, life-styles, and personal habits of a wide variety of people. My findings have been generally consistent. I offer these findings as suggestions—by all means test them for yourself. To do so, simply test-touch your thymus and have someone test your indicator muscle. If your thymus is strong, add the stimulus in question and retest the muscle.* If the muscle goes weak, then you know that the stimulus has interrupted the energy flow to your thymus gland and thereby reduced the energy in your entire body-energy system. Also, as I have already suggested, test in the clear. The double test is often important.

Let's look at a few common everyday findings.

Sunglasses: Looking through any form of tinted glass for any length of time weakens the thymus gland and hence the Life Energy. Test by putting on a pair of sunglasses. Leave them on for thirty seconds or more, and check the indicator muscle both while test-touching the thymus and in the clear. In nearly every case this produces weakness.

Wristwatches: Electronic pulsar and quartz-crystal watches often reduce the Life Energy when worn in certain positions. There are four basic positions for wearing a wrist-watch—on either wrist and with the face of the watch on the top or on the inside of the wrist. Generally, one of these four positions will *not* disturb thymus function. Try your watch in each position and see which one is right for you.

Hats: I have found that unless a hat is made of all-natural fiber, it will reduce the activity of the thymus gland. Of great importance is the lining, for many woolen hats are lined with synthetic fabrics. To demonstrate this, have your subject put on a woolen hat

*If your thymus is weak, strengthen it.

with a rayon or other synthetic lining. In the majority of cases he will test weak, either in the clear or on test-touching the thymus. However, if he turns the hat inside out so that the natural fiber is next to his hair and the rayon is facing outward, he will usually test strong!

This is but another indication that as we stray further from nature we are increasing our exposure to unnoticed potential dangers.

Wigs and hairpieces: Test your thymus; it should be strong. Now put on a synthetic wig. Test again. What has happened?

High-heeled shoes: It's unthinkable to enter a discothéque without wearing them. For years now, girls have been wobbling around in them, toddlers have been fascinated by them, and advertisements have suggested that gentlemen prefer them, along with the stockinged feet inside. They have gone higher and higher as skirts have been lengthened, and men have joined women in "going up in the world" on "platforms."

Everybody wears them, you say, *so what could be wrong with them?*

The answer is *plenty.*

The problem is that at the end of a walking step, when your foot is right behind you, the ankle is stretched forward in the same position as if you were wearing a high-heeled shoe. When we walk, sense receptors in the skin on the front and back of the ankle are continually sending messages to the brain, thus enabling us to coordinate our locomotion. When we wear high-heeled shoes, the brain is in effect being told that *both* feet are at the same time at the end of a forward step.

Thus, a double disorientation is induced in the brain. For one thing, we are not necessarily at the end of a step, and may, in fact, be standing still. Secondly, and quite obviously, it is impossible to walk with both feet at the back end of a step at the same time. This gross physiological disorientation causes great stress and leads to switching—a breakdown of normal brain-hemisphere symmetry. I call this imbalance the *stress of physiological disequilibrium*.

Obviously, then, the highest thing about high-heeled shoes is the risk involved in wearing them.

You might want to test another application of physiological disequilibrium. The next time you get in your car, have someone test you for cerebral imbalance with your feet in their usual position. Try various foot positions and determine which will be of most help in keeping you balanced while you're driving.

Synthetic clothing: A seamstress friend of mine told me recently that she entered a fabric store and immediately her eyes began to water, her nose became stuffy, she had difficulty breathing. She had to leave the store. Once outside in the fresh air, she recovered. I found on testing that the fumes from a recently unpacked shipment of synthetic fabric were the cause of her problem. The staff in the fabric shop had also noticed the ill effects of this odor.

For thousands of years we have clothed

ourselves with natural materials—fur, leather, cotton, wool, linen, and silk. Now suddenly we are confronted with many new materials—polyester, acrylic, nylon and various blends. I don't know why, but synthetic fibers impair the activity of the thymus gland and thus reduce the Life Energy. It may be because synthetics alter the normal ionization of the air around the body.

I always recommend that clothing made only of 100-percent natural fiber be worn. Certainly such clothing is available if you look for it. However, one area of neglect is women's undergarments. Synthetic-fiber undergarments, being tightly fitted, are especially detrimental. To test your own synthetic brassiere, start with a strong indicator muscle. Put your fingers on the outside of the cup of the bra you're wearing and have someone test you. Touching the bra from outside apparently has no effect. Now put your fingers *inside* one cup of the bra and re-test. Almost invariably your indicator muscle will be weak. The same testing may be done for panties. So here the two most sensitive, intimate areas of a woman's body are being adversely affected day after day by synthetic undergarments. The incidence of disease of the breast is alarmingly high. Is it possible that the cumulative effect of these stresses is taking a toll and tipping the balance?

What about sports clothing? It is discouraging to see so many people jogging and warming up in artificial-fiber clothing that is depleting their energy!

Bedclothes: Take a blanket or sheet of 100-percent-natural fiber, one made of cotton or wool or silk. Cover yourself with it and have someone test you. More than likely your indicator muscle will test strong. Now remove the natural-fiber blanket or sheet and cover yourself with a synthetic one. Test again. In most cases the synthetics will cause weakness. Even a synthetic-fabric umbrella held over the head is energy-depleting.

Disposable diapers: Hold an unused disposable diaper near your face with the plastic side out. Sniff the diaper. Does the indicator muscle go weak? If so, your results are no different from those of nearly every person I have tested. The same findings hold for most disposable paper products in your household. I have found that nearly all facial and toilet tissues weaken, and suspect that this is because they are treated with chemicals.

Toiletries: Test your deodorant. Apply it and see if your indicator muscle tests weak. Then test a chemical-free deodorant.

Madison Avenue says your brand of toothpaste is good for you, but what does your body say?

Test your perfume. Nearly all are synthetic and tend to weaken your Life Energy.

Metal: The effect of metal on the body was discussed in Chapter 5, p. 81.

Ice water: A kinesiologist, Dr. Robert Perolman of Florida, was troubled when some of his patients developed coronary occlusions after exercising. He found that exercise itself did not weaken the energy flow to the heart, but that ice water drunk after the exercising did! Test this for yourself by placing the fingers of your right hand one half to one inch below the point where the lower ribs meet. This is the heart-meridian test point. You will probably find that it tests weak after you drink ice water or take a very cold shower.

Lighting: BK testing nearly always reveals that looking at any type of fluorescent light is weakening, while looking at an incandescent lamp is not. There are many theories as to why this occurs. One is that the frequency of the light emission is either foreign to or harmful to the body. It was recently reported that animal tissues used in certain experiments had become cancerous after prolonged exposure to the fluorescent lighting in the laboratory.

I have also looked into the industrial applications of the effects of various lights, both in factories and in retail stores. I recently was asked to examine two women of middle age who had been working for some years in a candy store. For the past year or so they had been feeling tired and depressed and had had difficulty sleeping. But their most significant symptom was that each had recently put on about forty-five pounds in weight, nearly all around the trunk. When I saw them, they looked quite bizarre—they had thin arms and legs, thin faces, but very large abdomens. After a few initial questions, I determined that their troubles had started about a year ago when eight mercury-vapor lamps of 250 watts each had been installed to increase the brightness in the shop.

Both women tested weak under these lamps, but not when the lamps were switched off. Nor did they go weak when they put on a black hat. I concluded that the brightness was so intense that it penetrated the skull and was in some manner interfering with brain activity, perhaps through the pineal gland. This would explain the insomnia—the pineal gland responds to light and is the determiner of biological rhythms within the body.

I recommended that the women wear natural-fiber black hats while in the shop. One woman did, and the other did not. At the end of two months the woman who wore the hat for protection from the lamps had lost twenty-five pounds, her sleeping had improved, and she was feeling much better. The other woman, who did not follow my recommendation, remained the same as before.

After your own testing I think you'll agree that natural lighting—sunlight and candlelight—and incandescent lighting should be chosen wherever possible.

An interesting finding regarding lighting is that some people are so "borderline" that they seem to require the extra energy and tonification derived from light to maintain a positive energy balance. Under ordinary circumstances they test strong, but will test weak if blindfolded or tested in a completely dark room. As you can imagine, such people frequently complain that they are very tired in the morning.

Home and office insulation: One day in early spring I was testing a patient in my office as usual. Then it occurred to me to test that same patient outside. We went outdoors, just one step beyond the front entrance, and the previously weak muscle now tested strong! After careful investigation I narrowed down the culprit to the fiberglass insulation in my office, to which she turned out to be particularly susceptible. It was somehow blocking a flow of positive energy, if you will, from the "great outdoors." To test yourself for the effects of insulating materials, wrap some around yourself and then test your thymus gland. Almost invariably your indicator muscle will go weak.

Household fuel and chemicals: In the course of treating some of my patients, particularly those with psychiatric problems, I often investigate their home environment. In several cases I found that cooking gas adversely affected them. One woman would be cheerful enough when her husband, a kind and patient man, came home from work. However, as she began preparing dinner she would become argumentative, somewhat confused, and would cry. Eliminating her exposure to the gas also eliminated her "psychiatric" problems.

If you want to find out whether you are affected by cooking gas, just go over to the stove and see whether the indicator muscle goes weak first before and then after you turn on a front burner. It's as simple as that. Your body's answer is immediate and direct.

I also test for common industrial substances to which my patients are exposed. One patient brought in the bottle of solvent he was using on the job, which he felt might be affecting him. I opened the bottle and put it on the floor in the middle of the waiting room in which eight people were present. Each of them immediately tested weak where they had previously been strong. I advised him to change jobs. He did at once, with a dramatic improvement in his overall health.

It has been estimated that over 3.5 million chemicals have been introduced into our environment. Obviously, it has not been possible to test the safety of even a few thousand of them. However, there is one test that is safe and simple and can be carried out quickly, and that is BK testing. This should be used as a fundamental, primary screening device for any new item.

Smoking: It is a common experience for nonsmokers to get home from a party where many people have been smoking and find that their hair and clothing smell of smoke as strongly as if they themselves had gone through several packs that night. Thus, it comes as no surprise to learn that the harmful effects of smoking are not confined to the smoker.

If you want to find out whether cigarettes are harmful to you, just light up a cigarette and test your indicator muscle. It will go weak. Or have someone test your thymus, first when you are outside in the air, or even in a well-ventilated room, then after you go into a room in which people have been smoking. Almost immediately after entering the smoky room your thymus will go weak. In an average-sized room everyone will have the same level of nicotine in their blood within twenty minutes of one person's lighting up.

So deleterious is smoking to one's health, it affects not only the smoker but also those who come in contact with him. This is what we might expect. However, we would not expect to be affected by cigarette advertisements. Yet such is the case. Look at a picture of someone smoking. Your thymus will go weak! Your body is telling you something about the Life-Energy-depleting effect of smoking.

Auto exhaust: Do you want to find out if exhaust fumes are as harmful as they are said to be? If so, just stand behind the exhaust pipe of a parked car (not in the garage) and have yourself tested. You should be strong. Now, start the car, let it idle if you wish, and have yourself tested again, standing in the same spot. You will usually find that the thymus alone or all your muscles will go weak. The poisonous effect of exhaust fumes is thus quite apparent. And this is what we are filling our world with every day!

Sound waves: I will discuss in the next chapter how responsive the body is to music and to noise. One of the sounds with which we are commonly confronted today, particularly in large apartment buildings, is the sixty-cycle hum from electrical apparatus. Using audio generators, I have found that most people, until their thymus is properly activated, are weakened by this hum. I have also found, using these generators and sophisticated loudspeakers, that specific frequencies of up to 40,000 cycles and higher either strengthen or weaken the thymus. For example, at around 42,000 cycles there will be a general weakening effect, although the person tested does not "hear" this sound.

People also frequently test weak from the "whistle" given off by a television set, which is at 15,750 cycles per second. Think what is happening to you and your children if you spend many hours in front of TV: You are being drained of energy, not only by certain commercials and programs, but also by the sound, which may be inaudible, of this 15,750-cycle scanning frequency.

What a sensitive instrument the human body is, and how precise is BK testing! In my work with low-frequency sounds, for example, I have found that applying frequencies of two cycles per second to the body may weaken the thymus, but that three cycles per second will not; that seven or eight cycles may weaken, but six will not. When the thymus is adequately strengthened, these weakening effects do not occur. However, there are many instances when we are weakened from constant exposure to low frequencies.

These are the frequencies that warn animals
of impending natural phenomena such as
storms and earthquakes.

One way to protect yourself and your
Life Energy from these weakening, often inaudible frequencies, is to keep thumping
your thymus.

Magnetic fields; ionization: We are
constantly being affected by magnetic fields
around us. Even though this is not yet part of
so-called orthodox medical thinking, experimental work has shown that weak magnetic
waves can alter brain rhythms. In fact, the
body itself is a system of electromagnetic energy.

Our sensitivity to magnetic fields can be
demonstrated very easily. Place the north
pole of a magnet—say 1,000 or 2,000 gauss—
at the right ear of a test subject. (Why there,
I do not know, but I have found it to be a
very powerful point.) Almost invariably the
indicator muscle will test weak, an effect that
does not occur if the south pole of the magnet is tested at the same point. On the other
hand, though, if you place the south pole at
the left ear, the muscle again goes weak.

An interesting phenomenon revealed by
BK testing is that the biological effects of
foods, solid or liquid, can be altered by expos-
ing them to one magnetic pole or the other.
Even sugar exposed to a magnetic pole will
no longer weaken. Further investigation is
clearly needed, perhaps research in biological electron resonance.

The biological effects of positive and

negative ions in the environment are also just beginning to be appreciated. There is considerable evidence that our surroundings are depleting us of negative ions, which are vital for the maintenance of good health. Negative-ion generators are now available for purchase. A weak Life Energy can frequently be raised by turning on the negative-ion generator. If it is run for too long, however, the ion balance is disrupted.

If you want to test for ionization effects, get an "ionizing gun" from a stereo dealer. This device is used to remove the static charge from phonograph records. In most models, negative ions are emitted on squeezing the trigger, positive ions, on releasing it. How does it affect you?

There is what is called a nasal cycle every few hours, during which the body alternately uses one nostril more than the other. Goodheart has shown that taking the breath in through the left nostril negatively ionizes the air, and taking it in through the right nostril positively ionizes it. Under ordinary conditions the body balances the ionization as required by means of the nasal cycle.

The solution for the ionization problem, which is becoming increasingly important, is not ion generators, but good, clean, fresh air and correct breathing.

X-rays; electrical generators; microwaves: Millions of people and their belongings pass through security equipment at airports every day. In the rush, the questions we ask ourselves are: "Will I make the plane?" "Will I have a safe flight?" "Will that machine pick up that set of keys in my pocket?" "Will my ten rolls of film be ruined?" But how many of us ask ourselves: "Will this equipment harm *me*?"

I have not found any problem with the screening device through which we walk, but a considerable problem with the X-ray machine used to screen carry-on baggage.

Whenever this X-ray machine is operating, everyone within an area of ten feet will test weak, either in all muscles or just for the thymus. For everyone, though, there is a great decrease in Life Energy.

I am not sure whether this energy depletion is caused by the X-ray itself or by the electrical field created by the generator that drives the machine. This question obviously requires further study.

It may be argued that all this is not terribly important for us, because, after all, we are subjected to the machine's harmful effects for only a few minutes. We are subjected to many devitalizing forces for just a few minutes, but add them up and at some point they become too many and we take off on a downhill energy trip.

Think particularly of the person—often a young girl—who operates that X-ray machine at an airport for up to eight hours a day. She says with naïve faith in our industrial legislation: "My X-ray button indicates that I'm perfectly safe." If she knew how greatly her muscle energy was being affected by her work, she might have second thoughts about continuing in what may be a hazardous occupation.

It would be a great shame if in twenty years' time it is discovered that the people who operated these machines were adversely affected. Then all that will be said will be: "Tut, tut. We didn't know enough then to do something about it." *We certainly do know enough*. We know that any source of X-radiation and any generator of large, powerful electrical fields is likely to be harmful until proved otherwise. Until the laboratory tests are in, we can confirm our suspicions by using BK testing.

The effect of microwaves on the Life Energy must be considered. I have investigated the "speedgun" used by some highway police in detecting speeders. When pointed at an individual, this "gun" will sometimes cause him to test weak in the clear as far away as 100 yards. Microwave ovens that are defective or improperly used expose the body to dangerous radiation. Even when operated under safe conditions, they tend to decrease the Life Energy.

CB radios, which use low-frequency bands, also have an effect on the Life Energy, although only at a short distance.

Recently I was helping a friend choose a country property. He wanted a place that was quiet and secluded and as far away as possible from all sources of pollution.

The first place we inspected was desirable in every way except one: running down the middle was a transmission line of 18,000 volts. Although this voltage is low in comparison to that of large lines, my friend tested weak within 75 yards of the line. And this was the area on which he had planned to build his home!

The second piece of land we inspected was in a valley surrounded by tall green hills, beautiful and completely isolated, just as he wished. The property appeared to be ideal, and my friend smiled at his good fortune. Yet when I tested him he went weak. We looked around and soon spotted the source of the trouble: a microwave relay transmitter on top of one of the hills. My friend shook his head sadly, realizing that he could not buy the place, however beautiful, if the whole time he was there his Life Energy would be drained away.

Symbols: Many of the common objects in our physical environment contain symbols which go largely unnoticed. Through the techniques of BK I have been able to demonstrate the effects of hundreds of symbols on the body. Each affects a specific energy system. A few of these symbols have been discussed elsewhere in this book.

Paintings, which after a while blend into the background in our home or office, may contain potent symbols.* As an example let us take the Grant Wood painting "American Gothic" (see Figure 27). Have someone test

---

*In BK the study of the effects of visual images, particularly paintings, is called Psychoaesthetics.

Fig. 27. Grant Wood's "American Gothic."

you while you are looking at the picture. On test-touching, you will usually find that your thymus is weak. Now have yourself tested as you focus on each of the people in the painting. You will probably not be weak. But now focus on the pitchfork while being tested as you test-touch your thymus. What happens? Apparently, it is the pitchfork in the middle of the painting that causes a reduction in Life

Energy, not the stern-faced, darkly clothed figures.

I have experimented with variations on the pitchfork shape. A few examples are shown in Figure 28. Have someone test you while you are test-touching your thymus and looking at each of the variations, one at a time. In most cases you will find that it is only the true pitchfork shape, the trident, that has a weakening effect.

How is this possible? This shape is a symbol, and as a symbol is perceived as a gestalt, or configuration, that somehow produces stress. In fact, this symbol is an old one that has sometimes represented Satan and the forces of evil. Other symbols are beneficial. Test some for yourself.

Little did Grant Wood suspect when in 1930 he captured the Puritan spirit of the American farmer on canvas that his painting would tend to weaken those who viewed it.

A commonly viewed symbol is the cross. Now one would expect the cross to be Life Energy-elevating. However, in hundreds of clinical tests I have found that the kinesiological effect of the cross depends on the length of the vertical (upright) arm below the horizontal arm. (The length of the vertical above the horizontal arm is of minor importance.) Figure 29 (a) shows the Greek cross in which the vertical and horizontal arms are of equal length. This generally does not diminish your Life Energy. Test for yourself. Then test Figure 29 (b), the Roman cross. Don't be surprised if it weakens. Now

Fig. 28. Test your reaction to each of the following pitchforks.

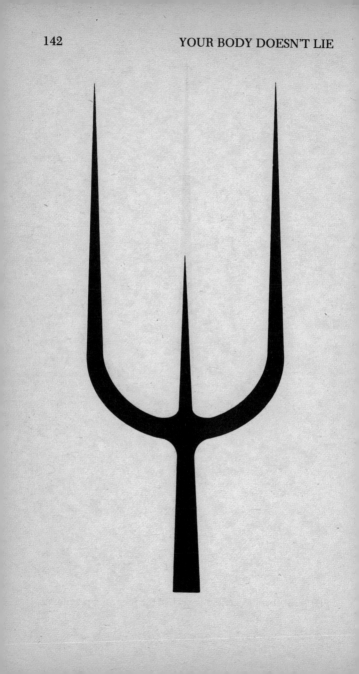

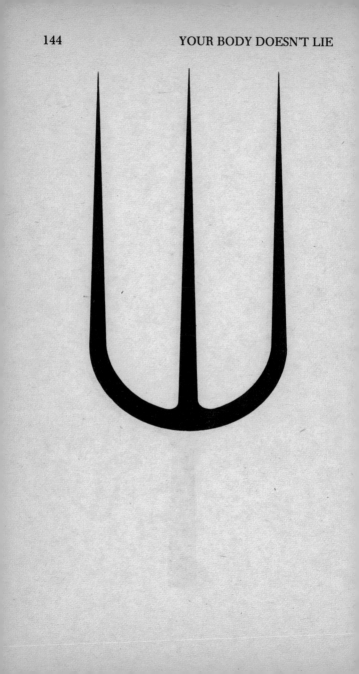

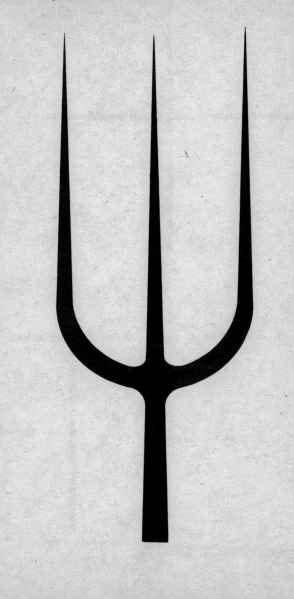

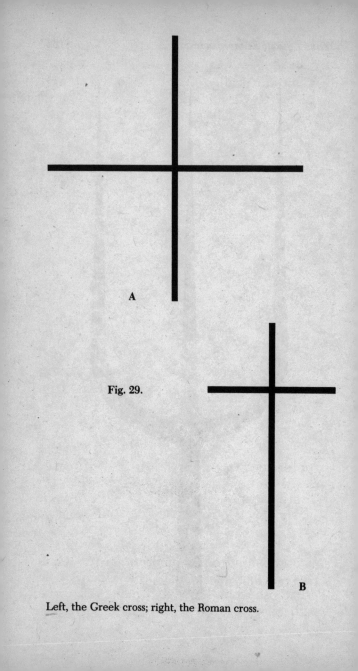

A

Fig. 29.

B

Left, the Greek cross; right, the Roman cross.

have someone test you as they cover part of the bottom portion of the vertical arm and gradually shorten it until it is equal in length to the horizontal arm. You will more than likely find that when the bars are equal, you will no longer test weak.

Another form of the cross is the swastika, a symbol widely used in the ancient world and through the ages. The word comes from the Sanskrit *svastika*, meaning "conducive to well-being." There are two forms of swastika, one that moves in a clockwise direction and one that moves counterclockwise (see Figure 30). The clockwise form was a common symbol for the sun, while the counterclockwise form often stood for night.

In spite of its recent use as an emblem for Hitler's Nazi party in Germany, the swastika is still a symbol of prosperity and good fortune. Even Jewish concentration camp survivors test strong in its presence, showing that this level of symbol response is deeper than the individual's experiential and emotional feelings.

Test yourself for the clockwise and counterclockwise swastikas. One or the other will make you weak, depending on which cerebral hemisphere is dominant. Of course, if you are centered, neither one will weaken you.

I have highlighted in this chapter only a few of the hundreds of environmental factors that bear consideration. Look around you. Test those things about which you have doubts.

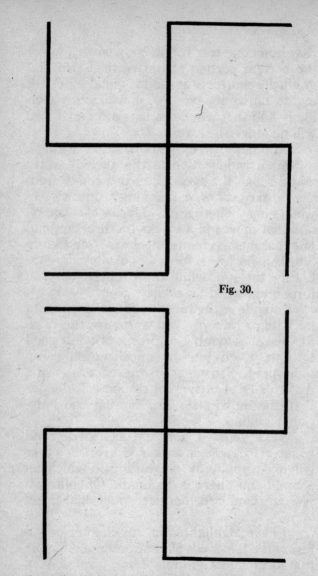

Fig. 30.

Above, the clockwise swastika; below, the counterclockwise swastika.

Fig. 31.

I have found this symbol to be very effective in balancing the hemispheres and thus reducing stress. I have therefore adopted it as the BK logo.

Now, in the course of testing you may find subjects (perhaps even yourself) who aren't weakened by a stimulus that is known to be devitalizing. Don't be concerned about this. If a person has more Life Energy than average, or is well centered, he will *not* be made weak by a negative stimulus that would weaken someone else. This is normal! Nearly all the adverse effects of the various factors mentioned in this book are manageable. When your Life Energy is raised, when your thymus is active, you should not be affected by these factors, either. And by following the guidelines of life-style retraining as set forth here, you will be well on your way to becoming not average but normal.

(9)

The Music in Your Life

"My pulse as yours doth temperately keep time,
And makes as healthful music."

—*Shakespeare*

I once met a pianist whose vibrant good health was striking. He was stocky but firm, and he carried himself proudly. Furthermore, although he was in his early sixties, his blue eyes were crystal-clear, his skin taut and unlined. The most memorable thing about him, though, was his *energy*.*

I tested him and found him to be as strong as he looked. What, I asked him, was the secret of his good health? Without hesita-

---

*Music is an aspect of our physical environment, but with such a special one that I have devoted a separate chapter to it and its opposite, noise.

Fig. 32. The Vital Life Energy of Arturo Toscanini. Test its effect on you. This is what he gave to the members of the orchestra for over seventy years.

tion he replied, "I eat good food, I sit up straight, and I have good music coming at me all day."

That very nearly sums up everything I am trying to say in this book. Good posture and good food are absolutely essential to good health, as are the healing qualities of music.

To the end of his long life, Arturo Toscanini possessed what musicians who worked with him have called an intensity, an inner fire, an electricity, a magnetism. His face was almost unlined, and the white teeth he flashed were his own. On the podium, he was vigorous and erect; when he walked, his step was light and buoyant. Into his seventies, he hadn't seen a doctor in years. It was even said that he sweated pure water!

The average age of death of the American male is 68.9 years. Yet at 70, some 80 percent of conductors are still alive and working. Following is a list of some long-lived and generally healthy conductors:

Casals, Pablo . . . 96	Stassevitch, Paul . . . 84
Ganz, Rudolph . . . 95	Stiedry, Fritz . . . 84
Stokowski, Leopold . . . 95	Böhm, Karl . . . 83
Mannes, David . . . 93	Coppola, Piero . . . 83
Panizza, Ettore . . . 92	Fiedler, Arthur . . . 83
Paray, Paul . . . 92	Harrison, Guy Fraser . . . 83
Boulanger, Nadia . . . 90	Dohnanyi, Ernest von . . . 82
Cameron, Basil . . . 90	Hanson, Howard . . . 82
Gui, Vittorio . . . 90	Pelletier, Wilfred . . . 82
Monteux, Pierre . . . 89	Beecham, Thomas . . . 81
Serafin, Tullio . . . 89	Hoogstraten, Willem van . . . 81
Stravinsky, Igor . . . 89	Muck, Karl . . . 80
Toscanini, Arturo . . . 89	Pfitzner, Hans . . . 80
Boult, Adrian . . . 88	Rühlmann, Frans . . . 80

Damrosch, Walter . . . 88
Klemperer, Otto . . . 88
Blech, Leo . . . 87
Ringwall, Rudolph . . . 87
Burgin, Richard . . . 86
Schuricht, Carl . . . 86
Wolff, Albert . . . 86
Ansermet, Ernest . . . 85
Heger, Robert . . . 85
James, Philip . . . 85

Polacco, Giorgio . . . 85
Strauss, Richard . . . 85
Szenkar, Eugen . . . 85
Walter, Bruno . . . 85
Inghelbrecht, Désiré . . . 84
Krueger, Karl . . . 84
Smallens, Alexander . . . 84
Slonimsky, Nicolas . . . 84
Knappertsbusch, Hans . . . 77
Konwitschny, Franz . . . 77
Kostelanetz, André . . . 77
Kurtz, Efrem . . . 77
Munch, Charles . . . 77
Talich, Vaclav . . . 77
White, Paul . . . 77
Amfiteatroff, Daniele . . . 76
Brico, Antonia . . . 76
Georgescu, Georges . . . 76
Kajanus, Robert . . . 76
Koussevitzky, Serge . . . 76
Lange, Hans . . . 76
Maganini, Quinto . . . 76
Marx, Burle . . . 76
Rossi, Mario . . . 76
Saminsky, Lazare . . . 76
Williamson, John Finley . . . 76
Abravanel, Maurice . . . 75
Jochum, Eugen . . . 75
Sabata, Victor de . . . 75
Schneevoigt, Georg . . . 75
Sevitzky, Fabian . . . 75
Wood, Henry . . . 75

Bamboschek, Giuseppe . . . 79
Barlow, Howard . . . 79
Chávez, Carlos . . . 79
Hasselmans, Louis . . . 79
Janssen, Werner . . . 79
Mengelberg, Willem . . . 79
Ross, Hugh . . . 79
Sokoloff, Nikolalai . . . 79
Wallenstein, Alfred . . . 79
Goldman, Edwin Franko
. . . 78
Golschmann, Vladimir . . . 78
Ormandy, Eugene . . . 78
Malko, Nicholai . . . 78
Steinberg, William . . . 78
Stewart, Reginald . . . 78
Weingartner, Felix . . . 78
Barzin, Leon . . . 77
Clifton, Chalmers . . . 77
Boepple, Paul . . . 74
Defauw, Désiré . . . 74
Ghione, Franco . . . 74
Horenstein, Jascha . . . 74
Konoye, Hideman . . . 74
Mravinsky, Eugen . . . 74
Plotnikoff, Eugene . . . 74
Reiner, Fritz . . . 74
Scherchen, Hermann . . . 74
Abendroth, Hermann . . . 73
Black, Frank . . . 73
Enesco, Georges . . . 73
Fischer, Edwin . . . 73
Szell, George . . . 73
Dorati, Antal . . . 72
Kletzki, Paul . . . 72
Molinari, Bernardino . . . 72
Sargent, Malcolm . . . 72
Coates, Albert . . . 71
Mahler, Fritz . . . 71
Barbirolli, John . . . 70
Karajan, Herbert von . . . 70
Dessoff, Margarete . . . 70
Van Otterloo, Willem . . . 70

Now, it is a well-known fact that the major conductors have lived, and are enjoying, exceptionally long, productive, and predominantly healthy lives. What is not known is the why, what, and how of it. Why do these maestros last so long in a world filled with heart attacks, strokes, and the degenerative diseases of old age? What is their secret, and how can we apply it to our lives?

These are some of the questions to which I have addressed myself for the past quarter of a century. My research has yielded some interesting answers—answers that have great significance for anyone interested in improving the quality of his or her life.

Through the testing procedures of Behavioral Kinesiology, I have demonstrated that our bodies can discriminate between beneficial and detrimental sounds; that our bodies can tell the difference between various performances of the same musical composition; and that our bodies can be helped enormously by certain sounds.

With the ears completely blocked, the body still responds to sound. This is because we "hear" not only with our ears, but also with our bodies.

Suppose someone has a weakness of a specific energy system or acupuncture meridian. If we block his ears and test the associated muscles while we are playing "good" music, his indicator muscle will test strong. But if, in addition to blocking his ears, we place pillows or other sound-absorbing material over the major meridian points involved, then the beneficial effect will no longer occur. The muscle will again test weak. However, if we keep those sound-absorbing pads on the points and then take off the earmuffs that were blocking our subject's hearing, with the music still playing, the indicator muscle will again test strong. Hence, we have separated hearing with the ears from hearing with the body. And often the latter is a better judge of what is good for us.

Our bodies have a pulse, and so does music. In a healthy state, we are in touch with our "inner pulse," which Dr. Manfred Clynes so well describes as "the key to the empathy we experience with a composer." "The inner pulse," he says, "represents a certain point of view. . . . Like a conductor's beat, a rhythmic alternation modified in various dynamic ways, the phenomenon of the inner pulse . . . is in effect an internally conducted beat."*

This inner pulse—so necessary to a conductor†—seems to be a key factor in his great life-span. George Szell, a famous conductor himself, once wrote of Toscanini: "Everything was pulsation and life from the first to the last note . . . you were completely absorbed in music-making and at one with him and with the composer." Highly attuned to this inner pulse, the conductor's every gesture reflects it. From Behavioral Kinesiology we know that each gesture we make is the body's response to a need to tonify or to cor-

---

*Manfred Clynes, *Sentics: The Touch of Emotions* (Garden City, N.Y.: Anchor Press/Doubleday, 1977), p. 78.

†With subtle BK testing, it is possible to tell if a conductor or soloist has the pulse and even to tell when he may have lost it during the performance.

rect an imbalance in a certain energy system.
A conductor is thus vigorously tonifying certain energy systems by the gestures he makes each day, at the same time that he is being flooded by the healing qualities of the music.

Surrounded by the right sounds, we all can be invigorated, energized, and balanced. It has been demonstrated clinically that music adds to our general health and well-being. Music, then, can be an important part of our program of primary prevention—the prevention of illness at a prephysical, energy-imbalance level.

Throughout the ages the therapeutic value of music has been recognized and respected. It is mentioned in the early writings of the Chinese, Greeks, Egyptians, Persians, and Hindus. Manly P. Hall, in a discussion of the therapeutic value of music, gives two interesting accounts of the use of music by the members of the Pythagorean community. One story tells of a jilted and vengeful lover who immediately surrenders his anger and malice when a Pythagorean strikes a series of chords on a lute. In another account, a demented, violent youth is "led away as though in a trance"* after another quick-thinking Pythagorean plucks a single chord upon a lyre.

Pythagoras himself was well aware of

*Manly P. Hall. "The Pythagorean Theory of Music and Color" in *An Encyclopedic Outline of Masonic, Hermetic, Kabbalistic and Rosicrucian Symbolical Philosophy*, 20th ed. (Los Angeles: The Philosophical Research Society, 1975), p. 82.

the therapeutic benefits of music. Hall tells
us that he "cured many ailments of the spirit,
soul, and body" by playing music specifically
composed for the sufferer. The Pythagoreans
began and ended each day with songs—
"those in the morning calculated to clear the
mind from sleep and inspire it to the activities of the coming day; those in the evening
of a mode soothing, relaxing, and conducive
to rest."

It has long been known how soothing
and at times invigorating the sound of running water can be. Waterfalls and babbling
brooks have always been good places for
meditation. The Alhambra, the Moorish pal-
ace in southern Spain, was constructed so
that the sound of water could be heard in every room and alcove as it rose in fountains
and fell from jets and the mouths of stone li-
ons. Now, you can't bring a brook or a water-
fall into your average house or your city
apartment, but you can always use your
shower.

If your thymus is weak, you will test
strong under the shower. This is due to three
factors: (1) the tonifying and therapeutic effect of the sound of running water, (2) the
stimulating effect of the water as it activates
all the acupuncture meridians of the body,
and (3) the negative ions produced by the
running water.

You will probably find that this therapeutic effect will pass soon after you come
out of the shower. However, it can be greatly

prolonged if you do the thymus thump and stand tall under the running water.

Let me give you a personal example of the beneficial effects of natural sounds.* When I found some time ago that I had to undergo surgery, I was apprehensive about entering the hospital, not only because of the surgery itself, but also because of the noise level of the modern American hospital—the sounds of machinery, of television sets, of people talking very loudly, of paging systems. After much searching, I found a Mexican hospital that not only offered the kind of surgical procedure I wanted but also had a charming and therapeutic setting. From early morning until late in the evening I was continually being tonified by the sounds of songbirds kept in the courtyard. I taperecorded these birds and have used their songs many times to demonstrate how healing natural sounds can be. Tape recordings of cats purring are particularly beneficial.

Several years ago my research on the effect of music took an unexpected turn. Shopping in the record department of a large New York store, I became weak and restless and generally ill at ease. The place was vibrating with rock music. Later I did the obvious thing—I tested the effect of this music kinesiologically.

Using hundreds of subjects, I found that

*This is part of the BioHarmonics program in BK.

listening to rock music frequently causes all the muscles in the body to go weak. The normal pressure required to overpower a strong deltoid muscle in an adult male is about 40 to 45 pounds. When rock music is played, only 10 to 15 pounds is needed.

This is far more serious than "just" a weakening of the thymus, which is, of course, occurring; when an indicator muscle tests weak in the clear, the energy problem is even more severe. As I have stated before, every major muscle of the body relates to an organ. This means that all the organs in our body are being affected by a large proportion of the popular music to which we are exposed each day. If we add up the hours of radio play throughout the world, we can see how enormous a problem this is.

Not all rock numbers have this effect, nor does a particular group necessarily have the effect consistently. Some groups and singers that tend to weaken our muscles are the Doors, the Band, Janis Joplin, Queen, America, Alice Cooper, Bachman-Turner Overdrive, and Led Zeppelin. In contrast, the Beatles never do. We must also remember that we are talking strictly about certain types of rock music. Rock and roll (which preceded rock), country & western, jazz, and other musical styles do not have this effect.

You can easily test your favorite records.

Test your subject's indicator muscle in the clear—that is, when he is not test-touching the thymus or any other point. It should be strong. Now play the record. If his indicator muscle is weakened, then the music has had a detrimental effect on his Life Energy; if not, it has done no harm.

If you need stronger proof that rock music is weakening, go to a musical-instrument store and find an electronic organ with an array of buttons that produce various beats (waltz, march, rhumba, fox trot, beguine, etc.). Push the rock-beat button and test someone whose indicator muscle is strong. It will go weak, just as it did when you played a rock record. The other buttons will not have this effect.

What characteristics of this so-called rock beat are responsible for this weakening effect? Careful listening to and examination of many rock records suggest that a common characteristic is a da-da-DA beat.* This is known in poetry as an anapestic beat.

This anapestic beat when clapped with the hands or tapped out in any fashion will produce the same effect as listening to the rock beat from the electronic organ or rock records. However, if the beat is played fast enough, this deleterious effect does not occur. Why is this? Now, one of the characteristics of the anapestic beat is that it is *stopped* at the end of each bar or measure. Rock music that has this weakening effect appears to have this stopped quality; it is as if the music stops and then has to start again, and the listener subconsciously "comes to a halt" at the end of each measure. The anapestic beat is the opposite of the dactylic or waltzlike beat,

*Not all rock music that is weakening has this beat, however.

which is DA-da-da, and in which there is an
even flow. This suggests an explanation for
the weakening effect of rock music. Of
course, there may be others.

In order to explain this phenomenon, let
us briefly discuss the internal sounds of the
body.

Arterial sounds can be recorded with sophisticated electronic equipment. When one
of my patients heard a tape recording that I
had made of the sound of his femoral artery,
he exclaimed, "My body is waltzing!" The
major arteries of the extremities do seem to
have a waltzlike beat. The heart sound, too,
can be considered to be waltzlike, the third
beat being tacit, or implied, as in LUB-dup-
rest . . . LUB-dup-rest . . . etc. Some other arteries have this sound, too. Thus, it may be
that when we are exposed to the anapestic or
stopped rhythm, a stress-alarm reaction is set
up that causes the indicator muscle to go
weak. The weakening rhythm is apparently
counter to the body's normal physiological
rhythm.

The old rock and roll beat does not seem
to have this stopped quality. According to
music critic Robert Palmer, "When rock and
roll is really rocking *and* rolling, it combines
an irresistible forward motion, a heavy
backbeat, and a certain lightness or lilt. . . ."*
Somewhere in the evolution of rock music,
the "roll" was lost.

---

*Robert Palmer, "When Is It Rock and When Rock 'n'
Roll? A Critic Ventures an Answer." *The New York Times*,
Sunday, August 6, 1978, p. 14.

I have found only two instances in classical music that produce muscle weakness. One is at the conclusion of Stravinsky's *Rite of Spring* and the other at the conclusion of Ravel's *La Valse*. In both cases the composer was attempting to convey chaos and has done it quite successfully.

La Valse begins as a typical waltz, but ends as a parody as it disintegrates into a crescendo of dissonance. Certain conductors (for example, Charles Munch) try to maintain the steady pulse of the waltz, and at the climax of these conductors' renditions, test subjects are not weakened. Other conductors, however, take a much more satirical view of the music (for example, Pierre Monteux) and deliberately break up the pulse at the end; here the subject's strong indicator muscle indeed tests weak.

Of the well over 20,000 records of all types of music that I have tested, only one other passage has caused the subject's indicator muscle to go weak, and that is one short segment of Haitian voodoo drumming. Nowhere else.

Thus, this debilitating effect, which has come to be known as the Diamond Effect, is almost exclusively present in modern popular music. As far as my investigations can discern, it first emerged in the early sixties. Since then this beat has progressed until it is now well represented in the Top Ten of any week. This infiltration of the music industry has taken place within only the last fifteen years.

What else does the rock beat do?

Using the principles and techniques of BK, I have also demonstrated that when the weakening beat is played, the phenomenon called switching occurs—that is, symmetry between the two cerebral hemispheres is lost, introducing subtle perceptual difficulties and a host of other early manifestations of stress (see Chapter 5 on stress). The entire body is thrown into a state of alarm. The perceptual changes that occur may well manifest themselves in children as decreased performance in school, hyperactivity, and restlessness; in adults, as decreased work output, increased errors, general inefficiency, reduced decision-making capacity on the job, and a nagging feeling that things just aren't right—in short, the loss of energy for no apparent reason. This has been observed clinically hundreds of times. In my practice I have found that the academic records of many schoolchildren improve considerably after they stop listening to rock music while studying.

The applications of these findings to industrial engineering are myriad.* One factory in particular, a manufacturing and repair plant for sophisticated electronic equipment, where concentration and clearheadedness are essential, was playing a great

---

*Of course, there are countless other human engineering and environmental considerations regarding the overall conditions in a factory or any other place of employment. I have researched many of these, but few are so easily changed and with such immediate and remarkable improvements as this.

deal of rock on its continual music broadcast system. It was recommended that this be eliminated. The management changed to different music and found to their delight an immediate increase in productivity and an equally pleasing decrease in errors, even though the employees were quite vocal about their dissatisfaction at having had their favorite music removed.

The fact that the factory workers so greatly missed the rock music is significant. The rock beat appears to be addictive; repeated exposure to it causes one to seek it. It becomes the beat of choice. It is as if the switching introduced by the rock beat has become the normal rather than the abnormal physiological state.

Furthermore, dancing to the rock beat causes switching because some of it involves using the same arm and leg simultaneously (right arm and right leg at same time, left arm and left leg at same time). Actually, the dancer is already switched by the music and adopts a homolateral type of movement as a result. (Refer to Chapter 5 on stress for a review of this concept.) The homolateral dance pattern then reinforces the switching.

Now, once switching becomes ingrained, as it were, a serious problem is introduced. The magnitude of this problem can be demonstrated by the following finding: If an average subject eats refined sugar, all indicator muscles will go weak. You have seen this yourself in some of your early testing experiments. However, if the subject is switched, the opposite will often occur—he will test strong with the refined sugar and weak with raw, unrefined honey! *It is as if his body no longer can distinguish what is beneficial and what is harmful. In fact, his body now actually chooses that which is destructive over that which is therapeutic.* In this light, consider the millions of people who are exposed hour after hour to rock music and are thus continually switched and stressed.

Turning down the volume won't help—the rock beat takes its toll even at low levels. This led me to investigate the effect of noise on the body. Standing on a street corner in midtown Manhattan during the day, a person is not weakened by the noise level. But when the level rises to eighty decibels,* as it frequently does, the muscle tests weak. Note that we are dealing with two separate effects. One (the rock beat) is concerned with a particular abnormal rhythm that weakens us irrespective of volume, and the other (noise) is concerned with a sound that will induce weakness only after a certain volume is reached.

In summary: Noise may be defined as sound which, when it reaches a certain level of intensity, decreases body energy. Detrimental music reduces energy at any volume. Muzak and most electronic music neither weaken nor strengthen. Good music and

*As measured on the A curve as commonly employed on sound-level meters. This is a critical level. Consider that 4,000,000 American workers are exposed to continuous sound levels of eighty-five decibels or more.

nearly all natural sounds strengthen at any level. But if you play good music so loudly over a sound system that distortion occurs, a level will be reached at which the sound weakens.

I recently made a most surprising finding concerning music.

Nearly everyone will test weak when they hear the isolated note C. Almost any C, on any instrument that I have tested, will have the same effect. With notes farthest from C (F or G), listeners will test strong; with notes close to C (A, B, or D), they tend to test weak; and nearly always, as I have said, they are weak at C.

I do not know the reason for this, but I could offer an educated guess. C has been called the "I am" frequency. It is said to be the home key—that is, the key with which we feel most at home. And it could be that when we are low in Life Energy, we are most affected by what should be the most basic and natural frequency for us.

If you really want to show someone that his body is in tune with the sounds around him, just play a note C and test. Watch the startled expression on his face as his muscle goes weak.

In this chapter we have seen just how beneficial most music and the sounds of nature can be. Your body's major acupuncture points are just waiting to take up these vibrations and use them to tonify your body energy system and raise your Life Energy.

(10)

The Life in Your Food

"Nutriment is not nutriment if it have not its power. . . . Nutriment in name, not in deed."

—*Hippocrates*

There are certain points on which nearly all nutritionists would agree. One is that the technological revolution has greatly altered the natural quality of the food we eat. Our foods today are more refined than ever before. And refining reduces or even destroys all the Life Energy in the food. Just as our bodies contain Life Energy, so do the natural foods we eat. But the more these foods are processed, the less, if any, Life Energy will remain in them.

Test someone's indicator muscle and find it strong. Then put a small amount of refined sugar on his tongue. Test again. In nearly every case* the indicator muscle tests weak, as does every other muscle in the body. Now give the subject some raw, uncooked, unfiltered honey. Test again. The weakness caused by the refined sugar will usually have been overcome. Not only is the honey not debilitating, it is positively strengthening.

And yet academic nutritionists say that sugar is sugar is sugar, that all sugar is the same. Your body says that this is not true. Your body is far more skilled a biochemist than someone trained in that profession. Your body says these are different. One raises your Life Energy and the other lowers it. One is dangerous, the other is not only safe to take, but it is also health-giving and energy-producing.

We can test in a similar way most of the processed food that, unfortunately, has become the mainstay of the American diet. Test bread made from white flour and white sugar. Then test whole-wheat bread, made with whole-wheat flour and without refined sugar. What a difference!

The problem with white sugar and white flour is the "refining" process to which the sugar cane and the whole grain are subjected.

*Sometimes a person who is switched will test strong with refined sugar and weak with raw, unfiltered, unheated honey. This paradoxical finding is hard to explain. If a person is severely switched (as frequently happens with a teenager who has been listening for hours and hours to rock music), it is almost as if some inner morality in the body has become reversed, in that the body actively welcomes the "bad" and rejects the "good."

Sugar companies and the bread industry speak of "refining" these natural foods, but the term is misleading. If I refine my thoughts, I am making them clearer, more exact, freer from irrelevancies and fallacies. If I, an amateur artist, decide to sculpt a statue, it will be far less refined than any Rodin work. In other words, in the Rodin there will be more detail and grace, and no useless clay. But what the food industry actually does in refining is take away essential nutrients until the food is in a storable form.

Some "food" is so draining of our Life Energy that the indicator muscle tests weak in the clear. Other food is less weakening; in such cases we test by test-touching the thymus gland. Test both ways before you are satisfied that a food is life-giving. The general steps to follow in food-testing are:

1. Test your subject in the clear and find a strong indicator muscle.

2. Have your subject put a bit of the food under consideration in his mouth, holding it there.

3. Test the indicator muscle again.

4. If the indicator muscle is weak, have your subject remove the food from his mouth and rinse.

5. If the muscle is strong, have your subject test-touch his thymus gland and retest (food is still in the mouth).

6. If the indicator muscle tests weak in the clear or on test-touching the thymus, retest to ensure that it has regained strength.

7. The subject should rinse his mouth with spring or distilled water before testing the next food.

Test your TV dinners, your supermarket ice creams and candies, your prepared cereals, your maraschino cherries, your alcoholic drinks, even your tap water. If you test weak, face the fact that continuing to eat them is destroying your Life Energy, putting you into a negative energy imbalance, and certainly not promoting positive health and primary prevention. After all, the purpose of eating is to gain energy from your food, so there seems little point in eating food that depletes it. But again, as always, test for yourself. Your body is the judge of what is right for you.

I find that artificial foods, highly refined foods, and processed foods usually cause you to test weak. On the other hand, organically grown natural foods will almost invariably increase the Life Energy. For example, if someone whose thymus tests weak eats a bite of an organically grown apple, he will then almost always test strong. Natural foods such as fruits and vegetables, grains, eggs, nuts and seeds, chicken, and most fish should test strong for you, unless they have been heavily sprayed or contaminated.

If you want to see for yourself how bad pesticides are, just spray some in the room and see how the previously strong thymus gland now tests weak.

Interestingly enough, if a nonorganically

grown fruit is eaten when your posture is correct, the detrimental effects are greatly minimized (see Chapter 11 on posture).

It is fortunate that your body can so accurately and instantly discriminate between "good" and "bad" foods. You don't have to ask the FDA or a biochemist; all you have to do is ask your body through BK testing. For example, you can resolve the saccharin controversy for yourself in a matter of moments.

How can we expect our children to eat better when they are constantly being bombarded with TV commercials and other forms of advertising that promote the tastiness and "goodness" of junk food? The simplest way to counteract this is to test the child kinesiologically, just as you would an adult, then give him some of the food in question and let him "feel" the difference himself. Children are very receptive to this testing, particularly when they recognize that if they stop eating the "bad" foods their athletic ability will probably increase. In fact, they are far more amenable than adults (hence all the TV advertising concerning foods directed at children). Adults usually raise all sorts of objections, such as "You're pushing too hard on my muscle!" They often don't want to learn the truth: that they are eating foods, ostensibly to gain energy, which are actually destroying it.

In the advertising world, food is said to be "good," as if it has some morality attached to it. And people say, "It may not be healthy

for me to eat it, but it certainly tastes good."
Most food doesn't taste as "good" as we think
it does; we've just been conditioned to regard certain tastes as being pleasant. Taste
preferences vary widely from culture to culture and are largely a matter of early condi-
tioning. In our society, our taste has been so
affected by advertising that it is no longer a
reliable determinant of what we should eat.

I have tested many food additives. All
weaken the thymus and even at times cause
the indicator muscle to go weak in the clear.
This is in keeping with research on the effects of food and food additives on hyperac-
tive children.

I remember twin girls, aged six, who
were brought to me as patients because they
were uncontrollable at school. They suffered
severe abdominal cramps and were behavioral disasters. In my office they ran around
knocking over the chairs, banging the doors,
and generally making abominable nuisances
of themselves. I showed them by muscle-testing how sugar made them weak and how apples (organically grown) and raw, unfiltered,
unrefined honey made them strong, and ex-
plained how this related to their athletic ability at school. They went home quite willing
to change their diets. All their mother did
was stop the obvious food additives and all
forms of refined sugar. She substituted natural sugars—fruits and raw, unrefined honey.

The twins came back in two weeks.
Their abdominal cramps had disappeared,
and their behavior had improved. On their

second visit they were model patients. In my
waiting room they were quiet, well behaved,
and in control of their energies. They had
gone back to school and showed their class-
mates how the soda pop and sugar made
them weak—and now the other children
were trying to swap their junk food for the
twins' apples!

A skilled practitioner may, through full
kinesiological testing, prescribe a comprehensive nutritional-supplementation program for his patients. How do the principles
of BK aid in this? As I have stated previously,
each major muscle relates to a specific organ.
Now, years of clinical trial and experience
show that specific substances—natural substances—enhance the energy and functioning of specific organs. Therefore, when ex-
tensive testing reveals specific muscle
weaknesses, the correct nutrient can be
given or prescribed. If the diagnosis was accurate, the previously weak muscle will test
strong immediately after ingestion of the
supplement.

Such procedures are beyond the scope
of this book. But certainly we can use simple
BK testing to find out what foods and supplements are beneficial to us.

If your thymus is testing weak, take your
usual supplements and then test to see
whether it has been strengthened. It probably has not, because while some of the supplements may be strengthening you, others
are probably weakening you. What you

should do, then, is test your supplements one by one, to see which ones raise your Life Energy. Of course, continue to take those that benefit you and discontinue those that do not. Often supplements are recommended for valid reasons, and yet the person will test weak on taking them. This is usually because the other ingredients in the tablet—colorings, fillers, and binders—are detrimental. One brand may therefore be strengthening while another apparently identical tablet under another brand name is weakening. So you need to test even the brands of supplements. But, again, let your body be your guide.

Which supplements are better—the highly refined or the lower-potency, more natural ones? Is, for example, 800 units of highly refined Vitamin E more effective than 4 or 6 units of more natural Vitamin E? The answer is usually the latter; the lower-potency, more natural substances are more likely to correct a specific muscle weakness than those of higher potency. The more refined supplements and vitamins may even weaken the patient generally. Again, test yourself and see what you find.

Chewing the supplements seems to produce a far greater response in terms of muscle-testing than merely swallowing them. Of course, capsules and certain supplements are not to be chewed, and you should always heed the caution regarding chewing that appears on the label.

I frequently recommend extracts of thy-

mus tissue for my patients who have
underactive thymus glands. However, of all
the natural supplements I have tested, the
one that seems to be the most strengthening
to the thymus and hence the Life Energy is
bee resin, or bee propolis, a resin secreted by
trees and then metabolized by the bees,
which bring it back to the hive to line the in-
terior. This substance is the subject of considerable clinical research in several European
countries, particularly Russia, Denmark, and
Germany. For many years it has proved to be
effective against bacteria, viruses, and fungi.
We now know that the reason for this is that
it activates the thymus gland and therefore
the immune system.

The role of food allergy in certain illnesses is well established. In my own experience, I have seen an apparently normal
woman eat some puffed rice and within ten
minutes suffer an acute psychotic suicidal
episode. I have seen ulcerative colitis pre-
cipitated by eating a small amount of zuc-
chini.

In many preventive-medicine practices
and in some psychiatric practices it is routine
to conduct food-allergy testing. Such testing
is a complicated and expensive procedure. It
can now be carried out very simply by BK
testing.

Just ask a friend to test you with samples
of all the food that you eat. Of course, junk
foods will generally make you weak. But if a
piece of wholesome, "pure" food weakens

you, then you are, for all practical purposes, allergic to that food at the moment. Over 90 percent of my patients test weak with beef, wheat, and dairy products. In allergies of any type, where the substance cannot easily be avoided, I find that there is marked improvement with enhancement of thymus activity.

I recently visited a man in a major medical center who was suffering from severe sensitivity or allergic reaction to a sulfa tablet given to him by his doctor. This had led to an ulceration of his entire upper alimentary and bronchial tracts, and it appeared that he would die. Through the grace of God, he lived. When I next saw him, a few weeks later, I obtained a sample of the drug and tested him and a number of other people. In each case, the muscle went weak as soon as the tablet was placed in the mouth, indicating that the person's Life Energy had been instantaneously reduced by this substance, and that under no circumstances should it be given to him because untoward reactions, perhaps, fatal, might occur.

This is such a simple test. It may not be 100 percent accurate in terms of correlating with other medical facts concerning allergies and sensitivities, but it certainly has as much intrinsic worth as any other testing technique. It is impossible to calculate the number of sicknesses and even hospitalizations, often prolonged, and even deaths, caused by adverse reactions to prescribed medications. Most of these could be prevented by this simple muscle test. Whenever you are thinking

of taking a medication, prescribed or not, just
place it in your mouth and see whether the
indicator muscle still tests strong. If the muscle tests weak, by no means should you take
the medication, for that would be violating
the basic dictum of BK—that if a substance
tests weak, it should not be administered.
You should immediately remove it from your
mouth and rinse thoroughly.

Your body has an innate intelligence. It
should be the final arbiter of treatment, not
the textbook or even clinical experience. If
the body's Life Energy (as measured by test-
touching the thymus gland) is strengthened,
then the substance may be given; if it is
weakened, then it should not. It is my hope
and dream that in the future all medication
will be tested kinesiologically before administration. Doctors owe this to their patients
and we owe it to ourselves.

Let us now consider the following famil-
iar but dangerous dialogue:

"Ah, a little bit won't hurt you. . . ."

"C'mon, just take one bite. . . ."

"Not even a sip? You can have one
sip. . . ."

With these words, diets have been
broken, alcoholics have set out on binges,
and people have been coaxed into poor
health, bad nutrition, and tooth decay.

For it turns out that even the minutest
amount of a harmful substance—say, sugar—
has the same weakening effect on the muscles as a larger quantity.

Now, in current medical thinking, dosage is all that's considered. We are constantly being told that a certain chemical may be dangerous, but that the amount we are exposed to or are taking won't hurt us. This is unproven. Furthermore, minimum allowable quantities are sometimes conveniently altered. Recently, for example, I read that a state governor came up with an interesting solution to a serious problem: A certain carcinogenic pollutant was at a dangerous level in his area, and so he simply "took care" of the matter, not by regulating or closing down the factories responsible, but rather by raising the acceptable limit of the carcinogen.

It's high time we realized that we don't know what the minimum allowable amount of a poison is. As long as a muscle tests weak because of a poison, then to no degree should we be exposed to it. *A poison is a poison!*

So get out of the habit of thinking: "Well, a little sugar won't hurt me."

A substance either raises your energy or lowers it. It is one way or the other. Something that lowers your energy in a higher dosage will not raise it under any circumstances. Do not get caught in a *quantitative* discussion. This is a *qualitative* issue.

We have considered the dangers of smoking in Chapter 8. This is a form of "nutrition" also, as we are ingesting the smoke.

Nearly half the American adult population smokes, in spite of the warning on the package. It is rare to find a heavy smoker whose thymus tests strong. The choice, of course, is up to the smoker—give up smoking and embrace life, or continue smoking and court ill health.

Test yourself and be convinced. If you smoke, tap your thymus two or three times to strengthen it. Now have someone test your indicator muscle while you test-touch your thymus. It should be strong. Next light a cigarette and take a puff. Retest. It will be weak. Often just holding the cigarette in the mouth, unlighted (not the filter tip, but the actual tobacco and paper), will cause weakness. It is difficult to get accurate muscle-testing results for other factors with a subject who smokes.

What a situation we are in! Billions of dollars are being spent each year to advertise junk food and cigarettes that only diminish our Life Energy. Our general food supply is getting steadily worse. It is more heavily sprayed and poisoned, it is more artificially cultured, and it is older by the time we eat it. And, on top of this, we usually overcook it to the point where no quality is left in it, no life is left in it at all.

It is harder for us today to find and prepare healthy, "live" foods, but we do have a choice. Once the difference between "live" food and "dead" food has been clearly demonstrated to us by BK testing, we should have no difficulty in modifying our diet accordingly. However, if we continue to resist such changes, our Life Energy has probably been severely weakened. This is, unfortunately, a common problem and is becoming even more common because of the enormous amount of advertising and promotion of unhealthy food.

However, let us end this chapter on a happier note. There is always something positive to be gained from BK testing. With the insights you develop, you will be able to apply the results of your own testing not only in the avoidance of what is "bad" but in the pursuit of what is "good."

Of course you have a choice!

(11)

The Importance
of Posture

" . . . our human upright Posture is a unique ac-
complishment . . . a most delicate poise and balance, an equation of forces brought about by an
interplay of the sensory and motor mechanisms,
by which all muscular effort is practically eliminated. The unique quality of the whole performance lies in this reduction of effort."

—*W. H. M. Carrington*

Biologists tell us that a significant mechanical
efficiency has been achieved in the evolution
from four-legged to two-legged locomotion.
Whereas it takes only 18 percent of a human
being's energy to remain upright, it takes
some 40 percent for an animal to support itself on four legs. But this figure of 18 percent
cannot be said to apply to the average person, who stands and sits with back hunched,

chest caved in, and head thrust forward. People with poor posture not only look bad, they expend a great deal more energy than they have to, whether they're standing, sitting, walking, or performing some task. They are continually fighting gravity rather than using it to advantage. If your body is improperly aligned, gravity will pull you in the direction in which most of your weight is concentrated. If each main section of your body—head, chest, hips, legs—is properly supported by the part below, gravity will actually help you remain upright.

Poor posture has other disadvantages that can be detected only through kinesiological testing.

Test someone's thymus by the usual test-touch method. If it is weak, have him sit or stand with his spine erect and his head up straight. Now the thymus that tested weak will test strong, indicating that the Life Energy has been increased. Good posture apparently facilitates the energy flow through the body. If your subject's thymus tested strong initially, have him slump his shoulders. His thymus will now test weak.

Let's perform another test. Have your subject eat a little refined sugar or some other substance that is known to weaken the thymus. If he is sitting erect, his thymus will not test weak! Apparently, when your Life Energy has been given a boost, your resistance to certain adverse effects will be raised. And correct posture is one of the most effective boosts there is.

Not only does poor posture interfere with thymus activity and reduce Life Energy, it also introduces switching, a condition in which the person is uncentered and there is an imbalance between the two cerebral hemispheres, as described in Chapter 5. We can test this in the usual way (see p. 72) by observing the difference when we test for cerebral imbalance when the subject's posture is "normal" (bad) and good.

Riding a racer-style bicycle or even an exercise bicycle may also cause switching. This is due primarily to poor posture, although the rigid position of the arms is a contributing factor. If the rider takes his hands off the handlebars and sits erect while pedaling, switching will not occur.

A patient of mine, a dedicated concert pianist, confided to me that he was finding it more and more difficult to read music and to execute complicated passages. We went to his studio and I watched him play. It was immediately apparent that he was sitting incorrectly, slumped over with shoulders rounded and head bent forward. Furthermore, his piano stool was so high that in order to see the music he had to duck and bob downward with his chin. In short, his posture was abominable! I tested him and found that in this position he suffered all the characteristics of switching—he was uncentered, he had a cerebral-hemisphere imbalance, and his thymus activity and hence his Life Energy were low.

I adjusted the height of his piano stool

and told him how to modify his posture. One week later he returned to my office with a grin on his face to report that his confusion and dexterity problems had vanished!

Factory workers may have a similar problem. In most assembly lines the work is positioned at such an angle that the worker is switched the entire time he is on the job. With careful adjustment of the height of the seat and the angle of the work, the cerebral imbalance disappears. Efficiency will then increase and errors will be reduced.

This leads to a consideration of the role of seating.

Metal chairs, such as the folding variety used in auditoriums, will cause nearly everyone to switch. (This is because it is metal crossing the midline.) So will modern upholstered chairs. Go through your house and test yourself in every chair. First, straighten your spine, satisfy yourself that your hemispheres are balanced, and be sure your thymus is testing strong. Then sit in the chair in your normal position. Test again. Now you are switched, uncentered, and your thymus is weak. All your soft, comfortable chairs are lowering your Life Energy and causing some degree of stress. Firm chairs with straight backs are eminently better. However, the most important feature of a chair is the seat itself. If you sit on a firm surface, your spine will automatically be straighter, your thymus will be strong, and switching will not occur. The stress on your body, and hence on *you*, will be reduced.

Desk chairs usually have firm seats and straight backs. However, most of us hunch over a desk to write or read. Obviously, the time when one is writing or studying is not the best time to be mentally confused and stressed. So sit upright as much as you can when doing mental work. And try not to cross your legs or feet, as this alone may cause switching.

Car seats can switch us, too. I recall a patient who complained that if he drove for half an hour he would become tired and confused and would start to misread traffic signals and directions. I advised him to sit on a firm board or sheet of hard plastic while driving. After that he was able to drive for ten hours and feel the same upon arriving at his destination as he had when he started—no fatigue, no confusion, and no stress. (So many people have difficulty orienting themselves with a map when they are in a car. Could it be because the car seat is switching them?)

I recommend that anyone who will be traveling by airplane carry a small, firm sheet of plywood or acrylic to sit on. This reduces fatigue and jet lag. I wonder how much of jet lag is due to disturbed biological rhythms and how much of it is due to sitting three, six, or even more hours on a plane, constantly switched, and with diminished thymus activity.

Pity the poor dentist. He used to stand all day peering into a succession of mouths from all angles. Now he sits on one side of the dental chair, his spine curved to some degree as he leans toward the patient. When he works with a mirror inside the mouth, he is oriented upside down. I have instructed hundreds of dentists to sit on a firm base and lean forward from the hips with the spine straight. Many of them have reported marked reduction in mental and physical stress as they work.

Dentists, hairdressers, salespersons, and other people who stand for long periods find supportive shoes essential. Certainly, it is hard even to maintain good posture if you are wearing incorrect shoes. Have yourself tested after walking briskly on a hard surface to see whether or not the shoes you are wearing are strengthening or weakening your thymus. If they are weakening, test other shoes. Also check the heel height. If your muscle tests weak when you are merely standing in the shoes, gradually raise the heels (or, occasionally, the toes) of the shoes by putting lifts beneath them until the muscle tests strong.

Swimming is excellent posture therapy. If you float on your back your posture will automatically correct itself because you will be free of the differential pull of gravity. Test to see if this strengthens the thymus.

A position for improving posture is taught as part of the Alexander Technique which was developed by F. Matthias Alexander. This is extremely beneficial. It aligns the body, therefore permitting a free flow of energy throughout and enabling the thymus to easily monitor and correct imbalances. This

Fig. 33. The Alexander Horizontal Position.

so-called Alexander Horizontal Position is as follows: Lie down with your knees bent, your feet flat on the floor, and the outside of your thighs parallel to your hips. Put some books under your head so that your spine and neck are aligned as in the figure (Figure 33). In this position you will be relaxed and receptive to all the tonifying influences around you, such as music. I recommend it to everyone as a daily procedure.

The first step to good posture is to think proud and walk proud.

Epilogue

"The great phase in man's advancement is that in which he passes from subconscious to conscious control of his own mind and body."

—*F. M. Alexander*

As you can see, the scope of Behavioral Kinesiology is very broad. It provides us with the means of assessing and evaluating the effects of nearly all stimuli, internal or external, physical or psychological, on the body. Furthermore, it gives us a new understanding of the comprehensive action of the entire body energy system. There is no area of life to which BK does not apply. It even sheds light on such diverse topics as instinctive behavior, the creative process, the origin of language, anthropology, ethology, the aesthetic experience, and modes of communication such as gesture.

In this book I have concentrated on only one aspect of BK: the effects of various factors on the thymus gland and hence on the Life Energy. If the thymus gland is underactive, energy imbalances in the body go uncorrected and the patterns for disease are set.

As I have shown, the major factors affecting the thymus gland and hence the Life Energy are those we experience in our day-to-day lives: stress, our attitudes, the people around us, our physical environment, the food we eat, and our posture. As long as we concentrate on the positive, beneficial factors in these six categories, the thymus gland will be active and hence will be able to carry out its vital functions. Only when the thymus gland is working properly is the state of positive health—not just not being sick, but being positively well—within our reach.

Throughout this book I have suggested a number of techniques for enhancing thymus gland activity and thus raising the Life Energy. Here they are for easy reference:

- Do the thymus thump three or four times a day to activate your thymus and reduce the effects of stress.
- Take frequent energy breaks. Recite a verse or two of poetry or look at a landscape painting (or a postcard of one). Thump your thymus at the same time to keep your energies balanced and minimize cerebral hemisphere stress patterns.

- Listen to revitalizing music. To prolong the effect, listen while you are in the Alexander Horizontal Position and do the thymus thump.
- Listen to the sounds of nature, such as birds singing and water running. Take a shower standing straight and tall.
- Develop a homing thought, one to come back to constantly, to help you stay centered. It may be a pleasant scene or even an image of yourself in perfect health.
- Keep your tongue on the centering button.
- Smile as often as you can. Do it several times during the day as an exercise. It will help correct any imbalances in your body energy system.
- Think and walk proud.
- Dwell on the positive thoughts: love, faith, trust, gratitude, and courage.

If you carry out these techniques regularly, you will be raising your Life Energy rather than depleting it. You will be able to glean the best from a given situation or circumstance rather than be dominated by its negative aspects. And you will be able to make changes in your daily life that will lead you to the practice of primary prevention.

Here are two important principles of BK:

1. *Test for yourself.* Ask your own body. Don't take anyone else's word for how something will affect you. Become your own health adviser.

2. *Choose those things for which you test strong; avoid those things for which you test weak*. This is the BK dictum.

In these pages I have given you some of my discoveries. There are millions more just waiting to be made. Go out and test, test, test. You now have the tools.

Appendix I:

Summary of the Major Functions of the Thymus Gland

1. In early life the thymus gland produces special lymphocytes called T cells. These are vitally important in immunological surveillance (the discrimination between self and not self, or between "good" and "bad"), which is directly concerned with resistance to infections and cancer.

2. After puberty the thymus gland's major immunological role appears to be the activation of the T cells by thymus hormones.

3. The thymus gland appears to have some sort of growth factor, as injections of thymus extract have increased the rate of growth in laboratory animals.

4. The thymus gland is involved with the strength of muscular contraction. In myasthenia gravis, a disease of the thymus

gland, there is generalized severe muscular weakness.

5. The thymus gland is involved in the flow of lymph throughout the body. The lymphatic system drains foreign matter, cellular debris, and toxins from the cells and carries them to the bloodstream for disposal.

6. The thymus gland monitors and regulates energy flow throughout the body energy system, initiating instantaneous corrections to overcome imbalances as they occur so as to achieve a rebalancing and harmony of body energy.

7. The thymus gland is the link between mind and body, being the first organ to be affected by mental attitudes and stress.

8. As has been known for thousands of years, the thymus gland is the seat of the Life Energy, the *thymos*. A healthy, active thymus gland makes for vibrant and positive health.

Appendix II

The Origin of
the Word Thymus

There is a strange irony in the fact that physicians and medical researchers could have found a clue to the function of the "mysterious" thymus gland in the meaning of the word *thymus*.

Although *thymus* comes from the Greek word *thymos* (θνμός), its roots go deeper. Tracing it back beyond the world of Socrates and Plato, we find that *thymos* is from the Indo-European root *dheu*, which is the base of a wide variety of derivatives meaning "to rise into flames," "to rise in a cloud," "to smoke." In Sanskrit the word was *dhuma*, from which come "fume" and "perfume."

Thymos was one of the most significant, complex, and elusive words in ancient

Greek. According to Julian Jaynes, *thymos*, or *thumos*, as it is sometimes spelled, together with six other terms variously translated as mind, spirit, or soul, was a key ingredient in the evolution of Homeric consciousness.*

In the *Iliad*, says Jaynes, the gods "told" men what to do and how to feel. In this first "objective" phase in the development of Greek consciousness, *thymos* meant motion or activity as externally perceived. But later, the gods' voices faded away, or displayed a fallibility that dismayed the mortals—and *thymos* became internalized (the second phase) and took on a more active role. Keyed up for battle, man strained to hear the commands of yore. From his stress came physical changes—a rise in adrenaline, a quickening of the heartbeat, and a corresponding "fluttering in the breast." In time, these internal responses to stress became associated with *thymos* itself. In the subjective phase of the evolution of consciousness, *thymos* was regarded as a "container" into which strength could be put. It was also personified. *Thymos* talked to man (and man to *thymos*); it gave him strength for warring and urged him on to love and victory. Thus conversant with man, *thymos* came to be compared to man, and given qualities that lifted it from the realm of *things* to that of *persons*. (Ajax may not have been anxious to fight, but his

---

*Julian Jaynes, *The Origin of Consciousness in the Bicameral Mind* (Boston: Houghton Mifflin Company, 1976), p. 257.

thymos was. And it was not Aeneas, but his *thymos* that rejoiced in victory.)

At one point in the *Iliad*, Achilles says: "Waking like smoke in the breasts of men, even as Agamemnon angered me, but we will let bygones be bygones, quieting the *thymos* in our breasts." Thus, *thymos* was metaphorically a rising of smoke in the breast, as its Indo-European roots imply.

In the second century, Galen gave the name *thymus* to the pinkish-gray two-lobed organ in the chest because, it is said, it reminded him of a bunch of thyme. But the thyme plant itself was so named because it was burned as incense to the gods. Indeed, the altarlike elevation in the center of the orchestra of a Greek theater was called the *thymele*, and sacrificial incense was placed in the *thymiaterion*, or censer. *Thymos*, then, was a rising of smoke, a burning of incense, a sacrificing up to the gods—all taking place in the chest, the inner altar. It was aspiration, songs of praise, spirit, and the putting out of love. It was the breath-soul, on which depended a man's energy and courage.*

So here we are, back at the beginning, recognizing the thymus for what it really is— the seat of the Life Energy—and at the same time incorporating the new scientific discoveries. This integration of the old and the new ushers in the Third Golden Age of Thymology.

---

*Richard B. Onians, *The Origins of European Thought* (New York: Arno Press, 1973), p. 50.

**For additional information on
Behavioral Kinesiology
write to:**

The Institute of Behavioral Kinesiology
P.O. Drawer 37
Valley Cottage, NY 10989

Regular seminars on BK are held throughout the country.

The Collected Papers of John Diamond, M.D., Volumes 1 & 2, and other publications are available through the Institute of Behavioral Kinesiology.

Also available through the Institute is *The Behavioral Kinesiology Report,* a monthly newsletter devoted to recent research findings and practical applications.

Index